# HEADING

## RUGBY FOR AMBITIOUS YOUNG PLAYERS

# FOR THE TOP

*Terry Head.*

Heading for the Top

# HEADING
## RUGBY FOR AMBITIOUS YOUNG PLAYERS
# FOR THE TOP

*Kerry Wedd*

*Foreword by Jack Rowell,*
*Coaching advice and contributions from*
*Brian Ashton and Richard Greenwood*

With acknowledgements for special assistance to Alan Barter, Michael Raw,
Dr. Norman Healey and Jonathan Wood. Contributions from Dean Richards,
Phil De Glanville, Rory Underwood, Mike Catt, Rob Andrew, Kyran Bracken,
Tony Underwood, Neil Back, Jonathan Sleightholme, Jonathan Callard,
Lawrence Dallaglio, Graham Rowntree, Grahame Dawe,
Martin Johnson, Ben Clarke and Tim Rodber.

International photographs by Russell Cheyne (courtesy of the *Daily Telegraph*)

**Quiller Press**
**London**

**Heading for the Top** *is for ambitious young Rugby players – 12 to 16 group.*

*The book looks at the skills and the learning necessary to achieve success. It offers encouragement and experienced advice from some of the very best players and coaches in the land. Every chapter is headed by one of the top England players – competitors who have had to strive to achieve such standards.*

**Heading for the Top** *shows that with perseverance, every ambitious young player can improve his performance. Above all, it underlines the enjoyment of being part of a worthwhile team game.*

**The Coaching Edition** *of* **Heading for the Top** *– is available by the same author. Specifically written to raise standards in the 12-16 Group game, the author includes coaching contributions from Brian Ashton and Richard Greenwood – both top line players and International coaches.*

First Published 1997 by Quiller Press Ltd, 46 Lillie Road, London, SW6 1TN

Copyright 1997 © Kerry Wedd

ISBN 1 899163 32 8 – paperback
ISBN 1 899163 35 2 – cased coaching edition

Designed by Jo Lee
Printed by Colorcraft Ltd, Hong Kong

# CONTENTS

# ACKNOWLEDGEMENTS

My sincere thanks to all who have helped to bring these pages together. I acknowledge especially the expertise of **Richard Greenwood** and **Brian Ashton** – both top line players and International coaches in their own right; also of **Michael Raw** and **Alan Barter** – former colleagues on the coaching team at Sedbergh – who have re-written parts of the text and made various suggestions. My thanks to **Jack Rowell**, to members of the **England Squad** and to photographer **Russell Cheyne** for their contributions to this project. I welcome this opportunity to express my debt to numerous coaches, colleagues, former pupils and parents whose support and friendship over many years has been so important; especially to **Jonathan Wood** and to **Sarah** for their constant encouragement.

Kerry Wedd, 1997.

*Photographs*
Senior players courtesy of the *Bath Chronicle*, the *Daily Telegraph*, the *Leicester Mercury* and Rhino Rugby. School boy shots taken by Anthony Moseley and Charles Price at Mount House School, Tavistock.

*Special thanks* to: Tim Buttimore, Derek de Glanville at Rhino Rugby, Charles Price, Headmaster of Mount House School, together with coaches John Symons and Geoff Whaley and their young players.

*Proceeds* from the sale of this book will be donated to **The Wheels Fund.** Providing modern facilities for disabled children, the project is undertaken on behalf of **SPARKS** and **The Lord Mayor Treloar School**, Nr Alton, Hampshire. (See back cover for further information.)

# FOREWORD

*By Jack Rowell*

*I am pleased to add a few words to this excellent publication for ambitious young rugby players seeking to improve their performance.*

*Our sport continues to grow rapidly. The arrival of professional rugby has brought many of the world's top players to our shores. The success of the latest British Lions Tour in South Africa will ensure further promotion of the game. For UK enthusiasts there is the prospect of World Cup 1999, with the final to be played at Cardiff. We have much to look forward to…*

*Rugby players today are taking part in a demanding, fast moving game – one in which the traditional roles and playing styles of forwards and backs have evolved and moved on. Our leading senior players now possess more uniform and interchangeable playing skills – underpinned by increased thresholds of physical and mental preparation. They are top class athletes in their own right.*

*With such an abundance of interest and enthusiasm evident, this young players' guide not only brings sharp focus to the game but also provides an update on key skills, knowledge and motivation. The material which follows has been drawn from a number of current international players and top schools' rugby coaches. I encourage all ambitious young players to study the contents carefully.*

*It is also well worth noting that, whilst striving for excellence, the book emphasises ingredients of fun, fair play and friendship which are so much a part of this game.*

**JACK ROWELL, England Manager**

Paul Grayson v. Scotland 1997.

# THE GAME OF RUGBY

> **"** To fully appreciate Rugby Union, you need to experience the lofty moments of success as well as the morale bending lows of defeat; you have to feel the hard graft of training sessions and to share some of the team struggles which unite players. With the onset of the professional game, players have had to re-double their efforts to improve personal fitness and the game has become faster and more demanding. Often it takes a deal of grit and

determination and unless you are willing to work hard at the game, you'll be wasting your time. If you are fortunate though, you will find yourself part of that special spirit which comes to a group or team striving together towards a common goal.

Rugby has given me many very good years. In the early days, as a working man with a young family, the game was never my whole life; I always kept other interests – and I think that this may have helped me to enjoy playing more than most. Rugby has been a source of much pleasure and many good friendships and I would certainly recommend it to any young person who is looking for a worthwhile sporting challenge. **"**

**DEAN RICHARDS**
**Leicester, England and the British Lions**

# YOUR PERSONAL APPROACH

> 66 *Before going any further, it is important to establish your personal approach to the game – your attitude, your temperament, your commitment. You need to determine just what you really want from rugby and just how much you are willing to sacrifice in order to achieve this goal. Each player must make his own decisions.*
>
> *For many young players the answer may not yet be clear. You will have various options and prefer to keep interested in a number of sports and other activities. You wish to enjoy your rugby but have not yet decided, finally, if this is the sport you wish to follow more seriously...*

Phil De Glanville at Twickenham

> *There is no urgent rush and many very good players do not take up the game until long after the age of 15.*
>
> *However, if you are ready to make your mark in the game, I recommend careful study of the sections which follow...* 99

**PHIL DE GLANVILLE.**
**Bath and England**

**HEADING FOR THE TOP** *contains advice and support from players who have experienced the international game; not so long ago we were all of us ambitious junior players like yourself. It is our hope that these chapters will encourage you to raise your sights – to realise that you can do a great deal to improve your game if you have the right approach...*

## i – SKILL AND FITNESS LEVELS

We must all start here. Certainly, you won't make much of this game without putting in a lot of work on your personal fitness and skills – and the sooner you can set yourself some clear targets the better... *(Chapter 3 on Fitness... gives a good outline of what you need...)*

## ii – DETERMINATION

No-one gets to the top, in any sport nowadays, without a deal of dedication. It has to matter to you and you must be willing to stick at it until the results begin to come. Essentially, you've got to enjoy the challenge of self improvement...

Steve Ojomoh v. Ireland. Strength and determination

### Just how determined are you to improve?

Are you a once a week player or will you put in the extra hours of practice to improve, whatever the weather? Are you prepared to work at it or do you expect immediate success? Are you easily discouraged or have you got the grit to succeed?

How determined are you?

## iii – TEACHABILITY

Some young players learn quickly – some don't; some listen carefully – some don't... What about you?

## iv – LOVE OF THE GAME

Some thrive on the competitive contest; on the raw challenge of pitting skills against others – your strength or endurance or cunning against theirs. Some thrive as part of a Team.

Jonathan Sleightholme v. Wales 1997. England's powerful winger on his way to score again.

## v – KNOWLEDGE AND UNDERSTANDING

It is a sound policy, sometimes, to put yourself into the position of **Captain** or **pack leader**; this way you begin to see more clearly the strengths and weaknesses which matter most; you realise that enthusiasm without understanding can be a real problem.

First and foremost, the captain's job must be to draw the best out of his players. At Under 16 level, he must accept that the **Coach** will play a vital role and that the successful partnership between player and coach is very important. Between them, they will agree the **Action Plan** – the plan which will determine how best to use the available players.

### Check List

Try giving yourself a score of 0–10 against each of the following headings… A score of less than 5 in any section is too low for an ambitious young player. Over 5 for each section would suggest that you are ready to read on…

| | |
|---|---|
| **Skill** | /10 |
| **Fitness** | /10 |
| **Determination** | /10 |
| **Teachability** | /10 |
| **Love of the contest** | /10 |
| **Support for the coach** | /10 |
| **Positive attitude** | /10 |
| **Sportsmanship** | /10 |
| **Understanding & Knowledge** | /10 |

# SUMMARY...

*So, back to the three key factors:*

## ATTITUDE – TEMPERAMENT – COMMITMENT

*What do you really want from rugby and just how much are you willing to sacrifice in order to achieve this goal?*

# ARE YOU FIT TO PLAY RUGBY?

**Including: A) Do you Know? – Ten questions on fitness,
B) Understanding Your Own Individual Programme, C) Test Yourself**

> *Ambitious young players must understand that the modern game demands new levels of fitness. This chapter is written for young players who are seriously considering more demanding training programmes.*
>
> *Top-line sports people realise the need for a programme which balances hard physical exercise with the benefits of developing mental strength, and a sensible life style. Any player who can learn to take responsibility for part of his own training will be taking an important step towards success...*
>
> *A pause here to ensure the right approach may save you hours of wasted effort.*

New Zealand All Blacks on Tackle Bags.

**KERRY WEDD and
DR. NORMAN HEALEY**

# A FITNESS GUIDELINES FOR YOUNG PLAYERS

**Question 1:** *Why do I need fitness training? I am a naturally fit person; I play quite a lot of games and I wonder if I really need any more fitness training...?*

**Answer:** Sensible question. You need to work at the right programme – but, certainly, all the other games will assist your fitness.

Your reasons for special fitness training are:
i) to prevent injury by increasing your ability to recover and by increasing flexibility.
ii) to build up endurance so that you can stay at your best, without flagging, for the whole game.
iii) to increase sharpness (speed, acceleration or decision making...)

**Question 2:** *Do I need to bother with special pre-season or out of season training?*

**Answer:** Yes. Most young rugby enthusiasts will enjoy a number of different games which will keep them reasonably fit. But Rugby fitness is not the same as, say, Swimming fitness or Athletics fitness. If you want to make the most of your Rugby potential then you will need a sensible pre-season/off-season programme which prepares you for the rather special demands of the game. Once the match season begins, you will be busy improving skills and team work; it is therefore essential that much of the hard, endurance training has been completed before your season starts. Senior players call this "money in the bank".

**Question 3:** *What sort of pre-season training do I need?*

**Answer:** Endurance work; flexibility exercises; speed training. (See **Individual Training Programmes** at the end of this chapter...)

**Question 4:** *I need to get bigger, stronger and faster. How do I do this?*

**Answer:** By following the guidelines here... Avoid the "get strong quick" adverts and learn more about the facts of how your body works. The essential point to understand is that your system needs to develop gradually – and the training programme must allow this...

*Now read on...*

Austin Healey (Leicester, England and the Lions) – one of the quickest scrum-halves in the game.

**Question 5:** *What about weight training?*

**Answer:** Heavy lifting work, weight training or repetitive "slog" training sessions are not recommended for the Under 16 Group. The basic reason is that until your bones have hardened or developed (usually at about 17 years of age) you can cause injury or upset to the growing process. Certainly, you would do well to seek expert advice before you include serious strength training in your private programme. In other words, concentrate on **Skills**, and on the recommended exercises for now. Strength training will be vital, but not yet.

**Question 6:** *Does this mean that I shouldn't drive myself really hard?*

**Answer:** Not at all! It simply means that you must allow recovery periods for your growing system. By all means, train hard and stretch yourself to the limit but (a.) allow recovery time and (b.) avoid slogging away for hours at strength exercises. Your policy should be to train hard for short, sharp sessions of an hour or so. Concentrate on skill and speed improvement at this age and save the serious strength training until you have stopped growing... As a general guideline: "If it's not fun, then there's probably a better way of doing it!" Take a day off after a really tough session and come back to it when you are fresh. In common with other top-line athletes, get your regular sleep.

## Question 7: *What about diet?*

**Answer: Good nutrition is important** because it helps you to recover between training sessions. You certainly do not need to become too fussy about what you eat but you may find the following suggestions are helpful…

i) **Eat plenty of carbohydrates** – the fuel foods. (Bread; rice; pasta; potatoes + fruit and vegetables. Breakfast cereals are good for you at any time…)

ii) There is good sense in **cutting down on fatty foods** and too much chocolate – but the key word must be "sensible" not "faddy".

iii) Variety in your diet allows you to enjoy your food and to get the most out of it.

iv) Try to take some water or a soft drink before and immediately after strenuous exercise.

## Question 8: *Eating before a match?*

**Answer:** Not a big problem. **Eat a little of whatever you like**.

Ideally, give yourself a gap of an hour or two before you play – but it's really a matter of finding out what suits you. You obviously don't want a huge meal just before a game! Once you have eaten, try to relax for a while, to allow digestion.

The old idea of "a steak before a match" ran into difficulties when it was discovered that it took 12 to 18 hours to digest! You would be better off with a couple of bananas, a sandwich and a muesli bar! Some players prefer toast and honey…

## Question 9: *Mental preparation?*

**Answer: I cannot over-emphasise the need for sensible mental preparation**. You have decided that you want to play well – so prepare for it. Teach yourself to concentrate before and during the match. Think about your role as part of the team. Get your mind alert to what may be required and, above all, be positive – not negative. Prepare yourself to achieve, not to fail. Give yourself a quiet period before the match…

Mental preparation takes the stress out of the moment, allowing you to concentrate, ready for what's ahead. You want to be relaxed but ready for action. There's no need for frowning and growling, over-aggressive threats or head-banging…

## Question 10: *Should I have my own individual programme?*

**Answer:** Yes. Every individual will be different. What works for others may not be right for you. Get some assistance when planning your programme – but the following guidelines may help…

What do you really want from rugby…?

# B UNDERSTANDING YOUR OWN FITNESS PROGRAMME

*Many young players will be forced to train away from the facilities of Club or School. You won't go far wrong if you include three types of training in your general pattern...*

## FLEXIBILITY • SPEED • ENDURANCE

*Where possible, train with at least one partner*

### I FLEXIBILITY

*Always start here...*

You are recommended to include flexibility exercises or stretching exercises every day – even on non-training days. It makes good sense to begin every session with gentle stretching in order to bring the muscles into use gradually. The "stretch" should never be savage – "mild discomfort" being the absolute limit. It must be a gradual stretch – not a jerk. Hold each position for a few seconds...

After a hard match or work out it is an aid to relaxation if you can spend a few minutes working through your range of flexibility exercises.

Flexibility – always start here.

Three of England's quickest. Nick Beal with Tony Underwood and Jeremy Guscott in close support.

### 2 SPEED TRAINING

There is no substitute for pace and all players should work to improve speed. As the competitive season gets closer, you need to "speed train" several days a week. You won't become a top-line sprinter over-night but you'll be surprised what regular, quality training can do... If possible, obtain the help of a qualified Athletics Sprint Coach...

Many rugby groups use "**Winders**".

On the Rugby field – **Walk** (try line to 22 line); **Trot** (22 to half-way); **Stride** (half-way to try line). Walk back to start again.

As the fitness increases, cut out some of the walking and lengthen the sprints. In early training, ensure that the "walk" sections are long enough to allow you to maintain quality in the sprints. Without quality, it's not worth doing...

Each length of the field is know as a "Winder". 20 hard Winders gives a good test of anyone's fitness...

You will read about top athletes using "bounding" or "rebound" training and this will probably form a part of your Club sessions when it can be fully supervised.

## 3 ENDURANCE

Your ability to keep going for long periods without losing your skill level. This endurance must be built up over a long period of time – months not weeks… It fits well into the off season period.

Steady running of 1 to 3 miles – several times a week. Run in pleasant surroundings if you can – on the beach or in the hills – but do it! You are building up basic endurance which will be vital later in the season…

*Targets should not be based on age alone; height and weight need to be taken into account*

### What sort of scores should I get?

Take the tests and record your own set of results. Your first fitness Target is to improve your own performance.

### But, be aware

It is quite usual to improve steadily when training sessions begin, but **be prepared to reach the first "rest phase" or "no progress" stage.** This is a period when many uninformed young athletes lose heart and believe they will never improve any further. Stick at it for several weeks and gradually you will work your way into the next "growth phase". Be aware that growing, like learning, tends to improve in steps – followed by rest periods.

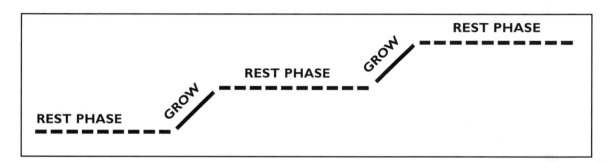

Training must be purposeful; it can also be fun

# C  TEST YOURSELF

*Your individual fitness programme.*
*Start by testing yourself on the five listed exercises...*

**You need to be fully warmed up before tackling these exercises**

### 1. The Shuttle Run – (Agility and Speed.)

- Take two points, 5 or 10 metres apart. (The closer the points, the more of an **Agility Test** it becomes…)
- See how many times you can "Shuttle" back and forth between the two points in, say, 30 seconds.
- Record your score. Rest for one minute and then repeat.
- See if you can maintain "good form" for 5 runs.
- Ideally, your partner will take turns with you. Time each other; compete with each other.
- But try to keep the rest periods to the same, precise time …
- As you get fitter, you can increase the Shuttle Sprint time or distance.

*We want "electric pace over 10 to 15 metres"*

### 2. Power Jump – (Leg power.)

There are two good Leg power checks:

i) *The Sergeant Jump* – an upward standing jump. Measure the distance between the highest point you can touch from a standing position, to the highest point you can reach with a standing jump.

ii) *The Mat Jump* – a standing mat-jump for distance.

- Lie on your back on the mat. (Heels right on the edge of the mat – not beyond.)
- Chalk mark the mat as far from your feet as you can reach with both hands.
- Standing jump from just off the mat. Measure the distance from chalk mark to heel.

*You should be able to leap your own height and beyond...*

### 3. Pull Ups or Press Ups – (Shoulder strength.)

It's very simple to cheat!
Decide for yourself what, precisely, you mean by a Press up or a Pull up.

- **Press ups** require a full dip to the ground. **Pull ups** require the chin to touch the pull up bar with no assistance from a body swing or a kicking action.

*Both exercises will give you a shoulder strength score to improve upon.*

### 4. Trunk Curls – (Abdominal or Stomach strength.)

There are numerous ways of measuring abdominal strength. A simple test is all you need.

- Lie on the mat. Using stomach muscles (not arm movement) sit up far enough to touch knee-caps.
- Lie back again – until head touches mat. Repeat sit-ups as many times as possible in 30 seconds.

### 5. Endurance Run – (Your ability to keep going...)

- Decide your own distance run – somewhere between one and three miles. It can be round a field or out on the cliffs…

**Time yourself over the run and then over a period of weeks, enjoy seeing that time improve.**

# KEEP YOUR OWN FITNESS RECORD

*Record your individual results and try to improve in one month's time*

Name

Position Chosen

|  | Date 1 | Date 2 | Date 3 |
|---|---|---|---|
| Age |  |  |  |
| Height |  |  |  |
| Weight |  |  |  |
| **1. Shuttle Run (Agility and Speed)** (2 points, 10 m apart) |  |  |  |
| **2. Power Jump (leg power)** (Sergeant or Mat Jump) |  |  |  |
| **3. Pull Ups or Press Ups** (Time limit of 30 seconds) |  |  |  |
| **4. Trunk Curls (Abdominals)** (How many in 30 seconds) |  |  |  |
| **5. Endurance Run** (3 or 4 laps of the field) |  |  |  |

# INDIVIDUAL SKILLS FOR ALL PLAYERS

*Including: A) Confident Tackling, B) The Skill of Passing, C) Taking the High Ball, D) The Defensive Fall, E) Play Touch Rugby League, F) Kicking Skills, G) Know the Penalty Laws*

## MULTI-SKILLED PLAYERS

" *Today's game requires all members of the Team to be multi-skilled. Backs must be ready to help their forwards with rucking and mauling; forwards must be quick enough and skilful enough to join the threequarter line whenever need-ed. All players should be comfortable about their role in attack or defence…*

*This section looks at skills which every up and coming young player should try to improve… and don't forget the Penalty Laws.* "

**RORY UNDERWOOD**
**Leicester, England and the British Lions**

## THE INDIVIDUAL CHALLENGE

" *The individual challenge of one against one is perhaps the most compelling reason for playing this game. This chapter lists a number of skills which can help all young players – but, remember, there's no substitute for superior fitness and sheer pace. If you are serious about becoming a top-line player – get yourself fit first…* "

**MIKE CATT**
**Bath, England and the 1997 Lions**

# CONFIDENT TACKLING

*In this chapter we have placed Tackling first on the list. Learn to tackle properly and you will feel confident to go on and build up all the other skills.*

*There are different situations when a slightly different tackle is required; where details are bound to alter slightly according to circumstances – but if you can concentrate on these essentials they will improve your game...*

i) Tackling is about **Timing** and **Body Position** every bit as much as it is about **Bravery** and **Aggression**.

**The basics include:**
Head up – eyes on the target.
Head behind; drive hard into the tackle; grip tight and hang on firmly until the man is fully down. Prevent the pass if possible; if the ball goes loose – we want it...
You must get to your feet before you can play the ball.

The tackle from behind.

**ii) For the more advanced tackler –**
Be in contact with the ground as you drive into the tackle. You want to be moving forwards and upwards into contact; use your studs to generate push, drive and lift. Aim beyond the man...
(By getting close to your opponent before the drive, you reduce the risk of being side-stepped or beaten by a change of pace. By driving upwards into the tackle, you are lifting your opponent and can then take control over how and where you want him to land.)

**iii) Practise** first with a tackle bag or a willing partner. Use matting and walk-through pace until you have really mastered the skill. Feel the difference between tackling from a distance (just out of range) and tackling from close. Feel the power when the tackle comes from leg strength...

**iv) Tackles to master –**
Tackle from the side – tackle from behind – smother tackle – head on tackle (shown below).

Confident tackling, timing and body position.

## B    THE SKILL OF PASSING

1. Power comes from the wrists – with the thrust being exerted by the flick of the two small fingers as the ball is released…

2. The ball should be held and received away from the body – to ease quicker passing…

3. Keep the ball always at finger tips…

4. Look at the receiver and pass a metre in front to allow him to take at speed and with arms away from his body…

Will Carling shows perfect timing v. Scotland.

## C    TAKING THE HIGH BALL

Every player is required to deal with the **High Ball** from time to time. It may come from the opposing kick-off or it may be that you are covering in defence. Usually, the **Full Back** or **Winger** will come from behind and call for the ball – in which case your job will be to give him immediate support, from behind.

**However if it is your High Ball:**

i) Get underneath it. Call "My ball!" loudly enough to convince everyone that you mean it. Try to turn side on to give yourself a really strong, wide base. Where it is possible, position yourself to react with a kick or a move but usually it will be a matter of staying on your feet until your support players arrive. Turn also to prevent a nasty knock as your opponent follows up. Catch with the whole body – not just with your arms. Cradle the ball and make it yours…

ii) The more advanced player will also wish to practise the safe catch high off the ground. This is more difficult.

Right: Taking the high ball. One advantage of taking the catch off the ground is that you should not be tackled while in the air…!

Only come off the ground if you know that otherwise an opponent will reach the ball ahead of you. You want the same strong, side on catching position – only this time you want it several feet off the ground.

Again, concentrate on catching with the whole body – not just reaching up hopefully with the arms. The key lies in making the ball yours and then coming down into a crouch.

As you land, you have to be rock solid and on your feet, ready for an opposing tackle or for your own supporting players…

iii) Practise on your own to begin with. Then get a partner to toss the ball and follow up, gradually building the pressure.

## THE MARK

A "mark" is really a defensive call, usually made by the Full Back or Wing man as the ball is caught. it must be called inside the defenders' 22 and is used when the alternative is to be tackled in possession of the ball. Both feet must be firmly on the ground as the mark is called. (A leap to catch the ball as in the photograph on the previous page is of no use if a mark is intended.) The referee needs to satisfy himself that the catcher is in full control – otherwise he will allow play to continue. Once called, the catcher should never assume that his "mark" has been accepted until he hears the whistle. Many a Full Back has been flattened after an unsuccessful mark…

**To mark the ball, you must have your feet firmly on the ground.**

# THE DEFENSIVE FALL   D

The ball is loose on the ground behind your players, probably not far from your own try line. You are the first defender to arrive. You have time only to hurl yourself onto the ball, just ahead of the attackers who wish to hack the ball onwards…

Much depends on the firmness of the pitch. If it is wet, it often becomes a "defensive slide" rather than a "fall". The basics remain the same – and apply to all players.

i) Eyes on the ball; back towards opponents; cradle the ball – pull it in to your body and then try to get to your feet. The law is clear: you must get to your feet or release the ball **immediately**. You cannot afford to give away a simple penalty.

As your skill improves, try to gather the ball and get up in one single movement.

ii) As you get to your feet you are almost certain to have to cope with an aggressive opponent who will try to rip the ball off you or turn you towards his own support players. Again, as with the **High Ball**, you want a strong, wide base which allows you to hold on until your own support arrives.

# E    TOUCH RUGBY LEAGUE OR SEVENS

I want all players to become skilful handlers; confident about giving and taking a pass and expecting to score tries… For this reason, I include **Touch Rugby League** in almost every practice session, whenever there is a gap in the 15-a-side match programme.

If you stick to the rules, it is a game which can be played with or without an adult referee. It can be played on grass, on tarmac or in a Sports Hall.

### Try the following basic rules:
- Non tackling. (Unless you have an adult referee.)
- Best with no more than 6 a-side.
- Touch on shorts or below. Two hands touch.
- Touched player must stop, roll the ball back between his legs.

- Player who picks up must pass immediately.
- Defending team must retreat 5 paces (or be at least 5 paces back from the break-down.
- Use the 22 or one half only.
- Agree the rules before you start! Appoint your chief official!

### Good tactics to encourage:
- Two quick passes away from the break-down.
- Insist on space between teams at break-downs.
- If the defending team does not retreat 5 paces – the game will not work!
- Always go forwards; make your support runners run off you.
- Keep the ball alive…

# F    KICKING SKILLS

Paul Grayson v. Scotland. One of the best kickers in the game.

All young players should try to become competent **Touch Kickers** but I also like to include **Place Kicking** as part of the **Skills For All** approach.

### TOUCH LINE KICKING

There are certain essentials to follow:
- Place the ball on your foot – don't drop it.
- Eyes on the spot you aim to kick.
- Head down – and keep it down – right into the kick.
- Follow through. Kick right through the ball.
- With care and skill you can add the **Screw** or spin to the ball – but the same basics hold.
- Practise both left and right foot touch kicking.

Head down…

16

Eyes on the ball – head down – good follow through.

## PLACE KICKING

*Make yourself into a top-line* **Place Kicker and** *you will be worth a place on most teams. It takes dedication and many hours of practice but there are a number of helpful guidelines to follow:*

Take care how you place the ball. Get right down, behind and low, when you line the ball up precisely as you want it. You don't need more than 4 or 5 paces for a run-up.

"Round the corner" or "straight through" kickers require:
• Eyes on the spot you aim to kick.
• Head down – and keep it down – right into the kick.
• Perfect balance.
• Follow through; right through the ball.
• Check the position of your stud marks after the kick…

Spend time experimenting with the best way of placing the ball. Try the different foot positions – toe-kicking through the ball or round the ball as shown. Study the experts…

## KICKING PRACTICE

Use a line for practice.
Kick for accuracy to a partner. Start close and move back as you become successful.
For serious practice/competition: use the Try Line. Try to bounce the ball back off a single post target. First to score 5 hits is the winner.

Excellent balance…

# G   DO YOU KNOW THE PENALTY LAWS?

**Why give the game away?**

*Few mistakes are more infuriating to a coach or a captain than those of a player who hasn't bothered to learn the Laws.*

**As an ambitious player, you need to ensure that you know what a referee must penalise...**

**a) In the Scrummage, you should be penalised for:**

i) not binding properly; you must have a genuine grip.

ii) deliberately collapsing the scrum.

iii) using a hand to help the ball out of the scrum.

iv) breaking away from the scrum before the ball is out.

**b) In the Lineout for:**

i) Holding down an opponent.

ii) Barging the opposition out of the line.

*ie. There should be no contact until the ball has been touched by the jumper... (At the time of printing, the Law does **not** permit **Lifting** at Under 15 level...)*

**c) On the Ground:**

i) Lying in a way intended to stop the opposition from winning the ball.

ii) Handling the ball again after you have been tackled. The Law says that you must first get to your feet...

*ie. If you're on the ground, you're out of the game. You must get to your feet before you play...*

**d) At the Tackle:**

i) High tackle. Neck or dangerous tackles should be penalised.

ii) Late tackle/Early tackle. The player must have the ball in his hands...

iii) On the High Ball. You may not tackle the man whilst he is still in the air.

iv) Obstruction. Deliberately blocking a tackler's way.

### e) Off-side:

Most penalties are given against off-side players.

In simple terms, **a player is offside in general play** if he is in front of the ball when it was last played by one of his own team. He need not be penalised unless he plays the ball or approaches within 10 metres of an opponent waiting to play the ball.

**A player is offside at a scrum** if he joins from his opponents' side. Any non-scrummager must remain behind the back foot of the scrum. The player putting the ball into the scrum is offside if he places one foot in front of the ball while it is in the scrum. Back-row forwards must stay bound until the ball leaves the scrum.

**Offside at ruck or maul?** You may not join the ruck or maul from your opponents' side; if you are caught out of position, you must immediately retire.

Any player not joining the ruck or maul must remain behind the back foot… (NB. at the kick-off…)

**Offside at the lineout?** Players not involved in the lineout must remain behind the imaginary 10 metre line until the lineout is over. (The thrower and the scrum half are regarded as being "involved"…)
The lineout ends when one of **four** things happens:
i) the ball touches the ground,
ii) the ball is passed back out of the lineout,
iii) the ball is caught/held, a maul is formed, and the whole "scrummage" has moved away from its original position…
iv) the ball is thrown beyond the 15 metre line.

*Penalties are so influential in the modern game that I strongly recommend players to list situations or incidents which resulted in a penalty either for or against. Learn to beat the penalty count and you will be a long way down the path towards successful rugby…*

Note that **Free Kicks** (**not** penalties…) are awarded for:

i) Closing the gap in the lineout too soon;
ii) Standing up in the scrummage (usually the Front Row who are in trouble…)
iii) "Not straight…" – in lineout or scrummage.
iv) Accidentally off-side.

Is this a ruck or a maul? see page 52, quiz 2 (3).

# IMPROVING THE HALF BACKS

## THE DECISION MAKERS...

66 *Half Backs provide a vital link for successful rugby; they bring together the threequarters and the forwards. Many of the most important team decisions come from this pair – to spin the ball wide; to break from close in; to take the ball back into a strong pack or to kick for position... Half Backs must be willing to take responsibility and to enjoy the challenge of directing the game...* 99

**ROB ANDREW**
**England and the British Lions.**
**Now Coach to Newcastle Gosforth.**

## THE HALF BACK PARTNERSHIP

66  *The Half Back partnership is crucial. It is a very demanding position, both in attack and in defence. At International level, things tend to happen pretty quickly and it is a huge advantage to be familiar with your partner's game – to know how the other man is going to react under pressure situations.*

*I particularly enjoy Scrum-half play because it keeps me in the centre of the action. It is my job to provide quality ball for my Outside Half, but I also share many duties with the Forwards. At any level, the more you can practise, and play together under match conditions, the sharper you should become.*

*Any ambitious Half-back will benefit from a careful study of the skills and practices listed in this chapter.* 99

**KYRAN BRACKEN**
**Saracens, England and 1997 Lions**

## i – THE OUTSIDE HALF

*You're fortunate if you have the ability to play in this key position; it requires a great deal of skill and dedication to reach the higher levels. Where possible, we will look for the running game, with the Outside Half as the man who sets his runners free. The secret lies in timing; in choosing the right option.*

It is commonly believed that **"great outside halves are born – not made…"** but here are seven guidelines which will help any ambitious young player.

 Take time to understand them.

i) The Outside Half moves as the ball leaves the Scrum Half's fingers – not before.

ii) Try not to run across the field. (You will remove space from your centres and also make an easy target for the opposing open-side flanker…)

iii) You want the ball into your fingers; in front of you without over-stretching for it.

iv) If you aim to make a break yourself – you want the ball flat; if you aim to move it wide, you still want the ball flat but you may pass the ball to a player who is deeper… (see diagram below Flat or Deep pass.)

v) Your running line should be such that you stop the first defender from moving sideways across the field. (ie. It is your job to "take out"/occupy the first defender…)

vi) For defensive purposes, you are often best placed directly behind your Scrum Half.

vii) Communication is vital. If you aim to kick, you will be almost stationary and your Scrum Half needs to know… Use agreed hand signals – not shouted instructions.

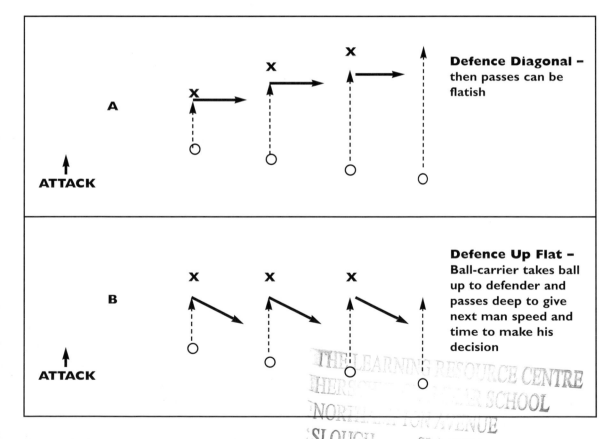

**A**

**ATTACK**

**Defence Diagonal –** then passes can be flatish

**B**

**ATTACK**

**Defence Up Flat –** Ball-carrier takes ball up to defender and passes deep to give next man speed and time to make his decision

*So much depends upon your opposition positioning. If the opposing defence is up flat on you, then you may have to pass a bit steeper; if the defence is well back then you can stay flat… Think about it…*

## ii – THE SCRUM HALF

*Make no mistake, yours is, perhaps, the most influential single position on the field. Not only will you need to possess more than your share of energy, skill and understanding of the game, you must also be a decision maker and a communicator. A silent Scrum Half is seldom doing his job; he must often be "the eyes of his forwards"…*

(Scrum halves need to practise as much with the **Hooker** and with the **Number 8** as they do with the Outside Half – see chapter 6C on Scrummaging…)

*Concentrate first on perfecting the really quick, standing* **Spin Pass** *off either hand; then work on the* **Dive Pass**, *to be used under pressure… A scrum half with the pace off the mark to make an occasional break is a huge asset. (Note: "occasional".)*

### a) The Spin Pass
- Start with a stationary ball and a stationary target.
- Aim to hit finger tips – at waist height – every time.
- Rear foot immediately behind the ball.
- Get low – over the ball, knees bent, eyes on the ball, weight on the back foot… Avoid backlift…
- As the controlling hand moves in behind the ball, your weight will shift into a good stride towards your target. (The other hand is merely a stabiliser…)
- The controlling hand stays in contact with the ball as far down the pass as is possible.
- Spin is imparted by pushing the control hand right through the line of the ball; it is not necessary to twist or strain.
- Be prepared to practise with and without the space/time for the back lift or pick up.

Andy Gomarsall v. Scotland

Spin Pass series.

## b) The Dive Pass

*The **Dive** puts a Scrum Half out of the game for an instant and should therefore be used only under pressure. (ie. moving away from fast closing opponents).*

- Start with a stationary ball and target.
- Begin several paces from the ball.
- First foot goes immediately behind the ball.
- Eyes on the ball for the pick up.
- Keep hands/ball back as far as possible before the actual delivery.
- Short pace before dive/drive away from opponents.
- Drive forwards and up. You must give yourself height to have time for a really accurate pass.
- The skilled passer will be able to develop a **Diving Spin Pass**

*A good example of the Dive Pass.*

## iii – COMBINING THE HALF BACKS

The Outside Half takes responsibility for his positioning and for the speed at which he wishes to move on to the ball. He must be in total control of whatever option he decides to take next.

It is the Scrum Half who must deliver the ball in the correct position, immediately it is available. Just as a Scrum Half wants no "bad ball" from his forwards so an Outside Half wants no "rubbish" from his partner...

The key factor involves the distance in front of the Outside Half that the ball must be passed. This is greatly a matter of trial and error in the early stages. Even at International level, however, you will find the pair can benefit from going right back to basics and rebuilding confidence.

## IV – TACTICAL KICKING OR KICKING FOR ADVANTAGE

Kicking away good possession is a last resort, but there are occasions when shrewd tactical kicking will bring the advantage...

With an inexperienced side, especially early in the season, it may be wise to try to play most of the game in the opposing half. To be sure, any pack of forwards will tell you that they prefer to be "going forwards", and this is the job of the tactical kicker. Obviously, we will want to make the maximum use of a strong wind or driving rain and to keep risk-play away from our own try line – and, of course, we may wish to kick to avoid opposing tacklers. The more the kicker can communicate with his own players, the better.

*There are 4 main kicks to master:*

### i) High kick into the Box
Usually from the Scrum Half, over his pack or line out, so that his players can drive forwards onto the ball. Often the Blind Side Winger will be able to chase and harry. (NB. He is crucial in putting the pack on side. If possible, he will be warned that the kick is coming.)

*This is an important kick to practise for a wet day ploy...*

### ii) High up and under (The Garryowen.)
Much the same as above but directed more centrally, usually for Centres to pursue and to put pressure on an isolated Full Back. Centres will try to get under the ball, catch it and make it available to the support players...

### iii) Diagonal Kick
Outside Half or Inside Centre kicks diagonally, behind the opposing Winger. If your own wing man is alert, he stands a fair chance of getting to the ball first.

### iv) Chip or Grubber

I don't like the Chip (little kick over opposite backs…) because it so often seems to give the opponent an easy catch and a free run. The **Grubber** (or push through the gap…) is usually more rewarding but it, too, is easily gathered or hacked forward by an alert Full Back. The Grubber is often effective on a wet or windy day when lofted kicks become unpredictable…

## v – THE KICK-OFF

Re-starting the game with a **Place-Kick** or a **Drop Out**.

*Coaching details will be as in KICKING SKILLS (Chapter 4) but it is worth re-emphasising the importance of this skill. Top line players spend ages working on precisely the right height and "float" needed for the chasing ball winners to regain control. It is a crucial and much under-practised area of the game… We should always be thinking in terms of regaining control from every kick-off…*

*Two practices to work on.*
**Practice 1:** place markers on the pitch and learn to land the ball exactly on the spot.

**Practice 2:** practise the kick-off with your specialist players… and don't omit the occasional, unexpected switch kick-off to an unmarked, speedy winger on the other side of the field…

Andy Gomarsall – high kick into the box.

A young player showing excellent balance in the Drop Out.

# THE XV IN ATTACK

Including: i) Threequarter basics, ii) Beating your man
iii) Forwards on the charge, iv) Forwards in close support

## A 15-MAN RUNNING GAME

66 *This chapter focuses on encouraging a 15-man running game and it welcomes recent change in emphasis towards this more open style of play by the very best World teams…*

*In years gone by, this chapter would have been called "Threequarters in Attack" but that would be to miss the important change in the game. Nowadays, we expect all our forwards to run like gazelles (or rhinos) and to be every bit as involved in attacking moves as our strike players. Forwards can be crucial in committing more than one opposition back to the tackle, so opening gaps or creating overlaps. It is all about team strategy, dynamism and speed of thought…* 99

**TONY UNDERWOOD**
**Newcastle Gosforth, England and 1997 British Lions**

## SUPPORT PLAY

66 *In recent years, the art of support play, especially by the forwards has moved into interesting new territory. Today's fitness standards mean that the game is getting faster. My job, as the Openside Wing-forward, demands that I am frequently the first support man; the person who must be close to the ball-carrier and in a position to keep the movement going. Support play is about linking backs and forwards in attack…* 99

**NEIL BACK.**
**Leicester, England and 1997 British Lions**

# ATTACKING MOVES

*Attacking rugby is what we all want to play – but it needs to be based on sound foundations. To attack without precision seldom makes headway. Our strike runners stand a far better chance of success if the opposition defence is disorganised, thus we need the team to keep working through second, third or even fourth phase ball in order to put a man into space...*

*Careful study of this chapter will help but, essentially, look for self confidence and the right moment to strike – key factors in launching attacking moves.* **99**

**JOHN SLEIGHTHOLME**
**Bath and England.**

# TOTAL RUGBY – THE OPEN GAME

**We hear a great deal about "15-man rugby", about the "expansive game", about "running rugby". Essentially, what every enthusiast wants is an exciting contest, if possible involving all 30 players – but there are a number of misconceptions...**

To outlaw the kicking game completely is to misunderstand the skills and purpose behind the tactic. Just as there is a time and a place for a back row move, a forward drive or a rolling maul, so there is the moment for a tactical kick. To run the ball "blindly" is a passport towards failure and is not the key to a more expansive game. Nine times out of ten, the exciting, 15-man game comes from a XV winning quick, controlled ball – often ruck ball – which allows the back division time and space... The key to Total Rugby is that all the players are multi-skilled; they have the ability to retain possession and to maintain an attack when less skilful sides must opt for safety.

**This chapter is about The XV in Attack but we must look first at a few basics...**

## i – THREEQUARTER BASICS

Make sure that every member of the Back Line agrees the following basics.

***Get into attack formation immediately***;
- Everybody takes their lead from the Outside Half.
- Be balanced as you take the ball – controlled, ready to sprint.
- Take early and use your fingertips.
- **Run and Pass with purpose**.
- Give your next man a bit more space or time to allow him to make his next decision.
- Pass at once unless you (or the next man) aim to break.
- ***You remain responsible for the ball until the player you have passed to has used it effectively.***
- Pass and back up at once.
- ***If tackled, it is your job to ensure that the ball remains available to your own side.***

## ii – BEATING YOUR MAN

The individual challenge of man against man is perhaps the most compelling reason we have for playing this game. Sometimes we use **Team Strategy** or **Moves** to out-manoeuvre opponents; sometimes we rely on our own natural pace, power or flair. Normally, we expect to compete against an **Organised Defence** (at First Phase) – and probably also at the Second Phase. However, if we can win Third or Fourth Phase ball we should be expecting to score…

If you have a man with electric pace or the power to break tackles you will want to use him. Team strategy is all about manoeuvring the opposition to give your strike players this split second opportunity…

### a) Switch or Scissors + the Dummy-Scissors
- Practise in pairs. One on the touch line; one on the 5m line. Walk it through.
- Receiving player must delay coming in as long as possible (ie. Don't tell your opponent what you intend…)
- Reach for the ball as it is offered. (The movement of the hand is often enough to convince an opponent that the ball is moving…)
- Ball carrier always turns towards the receiver; looks at him; offers him the ball. (Offer it; do not toss it.);
- Get close enough to deceive your opposition…

The **Dummy-Scissors** can be especially effective if it attempted soon after a real **Scissors** move.

### b) The Loop
Be closer than usual to give yourself a chance to move into position for the second pass. You can loop with the next man in your line or you can loop round further out…

Forwards on the charge. Lawrence Dallaglio running in to score against France.

### c) Draw a man and give a Pop-up Pass

This is all about timing – **and running straight**. Get on a line parallel with the touchline…

You draw your man by forcing him to come to take you; you do not want him to tackle you until your own support runner is in position and you may have to slow your forward momentum a bit. As your man comes through close and at speed, you will pop the pass for him to take. It may come as you are tackled; it may come as you are falling…

### d) Introduce the extra man

The possibilities are enormous but it needs planning. Blind-side wingers or swift forwards or the Full Back are all available to make the extra man but the skill is to surprise your opponents. The key is timing. When should the "extra" man begin his run…?

Force him to tackle you.

Draw your man and look for close support runners.

## iii – FORWARDS ON THE CHARGE

*Balanced XV's expect to attack from backs or forwards.* By and large we tend to use the forwards on the charge, to set up the second or third phase ball and disorganise the defence so that strike running backs can score. It is of course an unrealistic picture and every good forward will be looking for the scoring opportunity.

There are few more awe-inspiring sights (especially for an isolated Full Back trying to defend his line) than a pack of forwards on the rampage; skilfully interpassing and driving ever onwards at speed. It is enough here merely to emphasise the need for all forwards to practise the contact and close-passing skills; the quick rucking; the maul and the driving maul and to think very positively about your role in attack. Your first task is to win possession and for that reason your coach is sure to give early priority to set scrummage work and lineout work. That is essential. But after that – comes the main assault…

### When the forwards are on the charge

- In attack – don't fan out across the pitch. Preserve a narrow front. ("Get behind the number plate of the player in front of you…") You can call "left" or "right" as you accelerate to take the ball…
- Depth is essential to inject pace.
- Try to adopt an aggressive body position: shoulders low, high knee lift… Terrify the opposition!

*And get the ball round early as you approach the tackler. It must not be lost…*

## iv – THE BACK ROW IN CLOSE SUPPORT

One tends to think of Back Row players as the hard men who produce the "big hit tackles". Whilst this is partly true, a closer study will show these key players as vital links in attacking play.

Every good forward will be looking for the scoring opportunity.

The **Openside Flanker**, in particular, is expected to be "on the ball" at all times. If an Outside Half is looking to pass, he should know that his Openside is with him, usually close to his inside shoulder. The No 8 will not be far away and the Blindside Flanker, having checked his blindside duties first, will be close behind. It is true to say that the best Back Rows hunt in threes – and it is remarkable how often all three are involved in the final moves when a score is made…

Our aim must be to get men to the ball carrier or to the break-down point ahead of the opposition. Superior fitness and determination give a great advantage but there is no substitute for being able to "read the game"; to judge where the ball is going and to get there ahead of the rest. Many of the game's outstanding Back Row players have this uncanny knack and have built their reputations on this…

Support play can be rehearsed to an extent. The support runner can be told where the ball is expected to go so that he can get across and make the extra man. Back Row players can break quickly from a scrummage – or a Blindside Winger can use his pace to join the line as a support runner. It takes organisation and communication – but above all, it takes great skill to perfect the timing and the most effective line of running… Easily the best way to improve these skills is to watch an expert in action. Don't watch the ball; watch the particular player and see how he takes the best running lines towards the action.

Neil Back – specialist openside flanker.

England v. France, Twickenham 1997. Jon Sleightholme finds Richard Hill in close support.

Full Back Tim Stimpson in attack. Note the close support of England's powerful forwards: Simon Shaw, Jason Leonard, Tim Rodber and (right) Martin Johnson

# THE XV IN DEFENCE

## DEFENCE INTO ATTACK

❝ *Controlled and aggressive defence can be decisive in a close game. You will have studied* **Confident Tackling** *in Chapter 4. In this section, we are concerned with the overall team plan of defence…*

*Whenever possible, think of defence as an attacking ploy. Try to put your opponent down before he reaches the `gain line' (diag. p. 32). A well organised defence should be aiming to be first to the released ball and immediately turning defence into attack. I like to refer to 'attacking defences'…* ❞

**LAWRENCE DALLAGLIO.**
**Wasps Captain, England**
**and 1997 British Lions**

England v. New Zealand Barbarians. Lawrence Dallaglio stops his man.

## TEAM DEFENCE

❝ *All XV players must learn to be strong tacklers and to understand their role in the team's defence patterns. A totally committed defence can upset even the most talented of running XV's but it takes only one missed tackle to throw a match…*

*Often, the first tackle is crucial.* ❞

**JONATHAN CALLARD.**
**Bath and England**

## THE XV IN DEFENCE

The complete XV must be properly organised, to defend as well as to attack.

*Every man in the team has a defensive duty*. He must understand the key elements of *pressure, depth, cover and communication*. Controlled and aggressive defence can be decisive in a close game.

The following diagram needs to be understood by all players. You need to know about the **Advantage** or **Gain Line…**

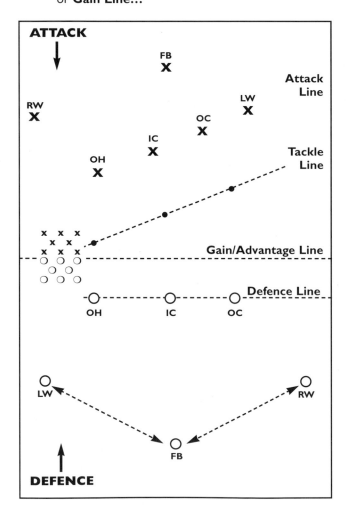

**ATTACK**

FB
X

Attack
Line

RW
X

LW
X

OC
X

IC
X

Tackle
Line

OH
X

x x x
x x
x x x
○ ○ ○
○ ○
○ ○ ○

Gain/Advantage Line

OH — IC — OC — Defence Line

LW ← ... → RW

FB

**DEFENCE**

### a) Defence for the Back Row and the Scrum Half

If opponents try a break from the scrum or the back row:

**On one side:**
Scrum Half takes the first man; Flanker, the next.

**On the other side:**

Flanker takes the first man; No 8, the next.
Aim low in the tackle and drive back over the gain line. *Stop the move before the gain line.*

Tim Rodber – Smother Tackle – v. Scotland.

**If the opposition goes wide:**
**Openside Flanker** takes the Outside Half (and continues to follow the ball across the field… running slightly *outside* each ball-carrier in turn). No 8 will be the next there, watching for the step back *inside*. The **Scrum Half** covers deeper trying to get between the ball-carrier and his own line…

### b) Outside Half and Centres.

Make sure you all agree the following:

i) Get into position immediately. Front foot just behind the off side line. (Back foot of the scrum; 10m at Lineout…) (Outside Half is responsible for setting this line…)

ii) Give your opponent as little space as possible.

iii) Keep inside your opponent. Force him to run outside you and thus into your strongest tackle line.

iv) Never go up ahead of the man inside you. The Outside Half should go up fast on his man – even if he then changes to a **Drift Defence** (and takes the Inside Centre…)

v) Start fast but arrive in balance for the controlled tackle.

vi) Agree to take the man who comes to you. If this policy is agreed, scissors or dummy scissors need not cause confusion…

vii) If your man passes, you support the player outside you. If your partner makes the tackle, your job is to get your hands on the ball. (Centres will often have to do this…)

viii) If a break is made **inside** you, turn with your man and stay with him.

ix) Put your man down. A half tackle which permits your opponent to get the ball away, must count as a failure. If you can, turn him so that the ball is where we want it, on our side.

x) After the tackle, get away from man and ball. Get up before you play it. Don't be penalised…

## c) The Full Back and the Wingers. (The Back Three…)

The back three must work together to provide depth in defence. They also have the job of setting up many of the counter-attacks. When the ball is in the air, one player should call for it. If in any doubt, the player who is deeper should take it and the other two should get round behind him to give support or start the counter attack.

The **Full Back** is the central defender. As a rough guide, he should be in line with the opposition ball carrier and in a position where he can if necessary force that player to the outside… It is far easier to move forwards into the catch or the tackle and under no circumstances should you get too close. If you have to deal with a ball in the air, do everything you can to take it before it bounces… Never flyhack!

The **Openside Wing** has to balance his two jobs. He must be ready to get up fast and pressurise his opposition winger but he must also be alert to the long diagonal kick from their Outside Half or Inside Centre… As the Openside Wing moves up on his man, the Full Back will move across to cover and the Blindside Wing will drop deeper to cover the Full Back. The three work together and build confidence by frequent communication…

The **Blindside Wing** has a particularly difficult defensive role on the "narrow side" near his own line. He must be quite clear – along with his Scrum Half and Back Row – whether he should come in and take the man in possession, or stay out and take his own man. This must be agreed before the game… Normally, he should stay with his own man unless an opponent has a certain score…

## d) Forward Cover Lines

Team defence requires every player to take part. Remember we are attacking their ball-carrier, retrieving the ball and then being in position to counter-attack. It takes great discipline and determination to get into position and it is essential not to waste energy by running the wrong lines…

**Guidelines would include:**

i) Get between the ball and your own line – quickly. Don't just follow the ball…

ii) If you are covering across the field, assume that the outside opponent will receive the ball. The first tackler must keep going out, knowing that anyone coming inside him will be taken by his next player…

iii) Keep your head up and watch play develop (ie. If a ruck has been won, head for the next likely breakdown. Anticipate play and get there…)

Will Greenwood, Leicester and the British Lions. A player to watch…

**Don't try to play the game going backwards under pressure**

**Kill the loose ball**

**Set up a maul**

**Get organised**

**and then PLAY RUGBY.**

# EIGHT

# SCRUMMAGING

## THE IMPORTANCE OF THE FRONT FIVE

**66** *It is not by chance that most successful teams can look towards the foundation of a power-ful Front Five. Even with the Law changes – especially in the U.19 game (p 50. Quiz 4) – scrummaging remains vitally important. There is a psychological advantage gained by being part of the stronger pack and this undoubtedly influences the rest of the team.*

*Today's Front Five must be quick around the field – ready to get involved in defence and support play – like every other player in the team.*

*Front Five play, however, is not for everyone! It's an area of severe strain and constant knocks and if you aren't ready to compete, I'd leave it alone. You've got to enjoy a bit of a battle really!* **99**

**GRAHAM ROWNTREE**
**Leicester, England and 1997 British Lions.**

England v. Scotland 1997.

# SCRUMMAGE DIAGRAMS AND CHECK POINTS   A

## I – PUSHING POSITION

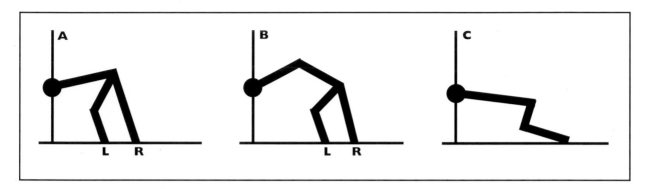

**You want position C.**
Hips below shoulders.
Chin forward to straighten back.
90 degrees between trunk and thighs.
90 degrees between thighs and lower leg.
Knees low.
Bind tight. Pull hard on waist bands and jerseys. Get tighter and lower than your opponents.

England team training. Note the flat spines – feet well back – heads up.

## 2 – STABILITY AND POWER

Feet wide, a little more than shoulder width (except for the Loose-head Prop who will be wider...) *This gives stability and allows use and transfer of power...*
Use your front 4 or 6 studs...

- Try to arch your back – hollow if possible. *This will straighten your spine to allow transfer of power/shove from behind.*
- Get as braced and tight as possible.
- **Look up! Look through your own scrum.** If you are staring at the grass – you're in the wrong position...
- **Force your head up.**

## 3 – TRANSFER OF POWER

The spines must be in line.
- **Start low**.
- Hips below shoulders.
- Get trunk lower by getting your knees nearer the ground. (Keep feet in the 90 degree position.)
- **On the 8-man drive** – get even lower.
- **If a Prop is in trouble** – get the hips lower and expect more support from your Wing Forward...

Jack Rowell supervising England.

Beware of this position – the Prop will 'pop out'

## 4 – THE DRIVE

- At the moment of drive, drop the knees a little lower.
- Pick your head up and concentrate on driving **forwards and up**...
- Spine not merely flat, but depressed in the middle. Backside pushed out and back.
- "Squeeze! Knees! Now!"
- Try to direct the drive **inwards** towards the centre of the scrum, without impeding your hooker...

## 5 – THE LOCK OUT

- On your own ball concentrate on the **Lock Out**; don't go backwards.
- Hooker strikes and everyone else...
- Drives into the locked position – and stays there.
- From here, your pack leader can call for a secondary drive...

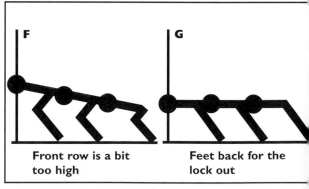

Front row is a bit too high

Feet back for the lock out

## 6 – THE FRONT ROW

### 6. THE FRONT ROW.

Shoulder height of the Front Row is vital. Get underneath...
*(The Law requires that you do not "take the scrum down" but you want to try to get below your opponents and drive up into them...)*
*(Arm and neck strength – as well as lower body strength – is vital here.)*

**Tight Head** leads into the scrummage.
**Loose Head** keeps the scrum high enough for the Hooker to see.
**Tight Head** stays low to restrict the view of their Hooker.

## 7 – ON THEIR BALL

- Get even lower.
- Eight men get feet back and drive.
- Flankers pack down straighter to assist forward momentum.
- Once in a while, the **Hooker** should have a go "*against the head*" but, essentially, you are aiming to give your opposing Scrum Half the worst ball possible.

If we can pinch the ball against the head, we will usually go for a No 8 pick up …

## 8 – BINDING

"Let's see the whites of your knuckles!" Get tight and then tighter…
Use the commands "Squeeze! Knees! Now!"
Re-tighten binding after initial contact with the opposition. Tight Head call "tighten" as soon as packs are down…
As the ball comes in, pull forwards on your colleagues' waist bands. Use your arm power!

### YOU MAY NOT…

1. **Kick the ball out of the tunnel**
2. **Handle the ball in the scrum**
**(unless for a Push Over try…)**
3. **Deliberately collapse the scrum**
4. **Deliberately fall or kneel in the scrum**
5. **Deliberately lift an opponent off his feet**
6. **Leave the scrum until the ball is out**

Front Row. Good, wide position of the Loose Head.

# B   THE JOB OF THE HOOKER

The Hooker.

## QUOTES FROM THE HOOKER...

 *Hookers must be very competitive. A single ball lost, on our own put in, is a serious error...*
*Fitness is the key. The fitter man will always come out on top...*
*I seldom strike for the ball on their put in, usually we are concentrating on an 8-man drive and I think of myself as a third Prop...*
*Speed around the field is becoming more important. I have to train as an extra Flanker and expect to be heavily involved in support play and in defence...* **99**

**GRAHAM DAWE – Bath and England.**

Bath pack in action.

### Channel 1
For quick ball – but it puts your Scrum Half under pressure.

### Channel 2
Controlled by No.8 + Scrum Half.
The normal route...

### Hooker practice
Relax the striking leg; take all the weight off it.
Strike with the speed of a cobra! Aim beyond the ball.
Guide the ball back to your Scrum Half or No.8.

### "A Hooker is no better than his Props..."
Work/talk with your Props every session. If they can put pressure on the opposing Hooker and upon the opposing binding – your life is that much easier.

**Work with your Scrum Half** to agree exactly how you want the ball put into the scrum. You need a code between you – probably just a movement of the hand...

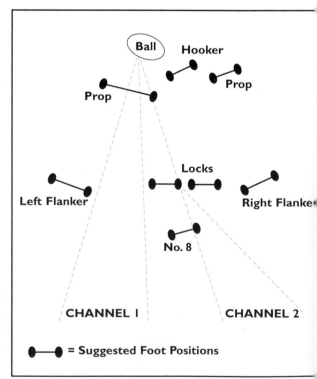

# THE SCRUMMAGING BACK ROW     C

*Page 29/30 examines the Back Row in Attack.*
*Page 32 looks at Defensive duties.*
*Here, we consider the work at the Scrummage…*

***Back Row scrummaging must be a sensitive balance between:***
***i) staying low and adding 100% support to the forward drive;***
***ii) staying low and helping to prevent any backward movement (the lock out);***
***iii) preparing to break – either in attack or defence.***

Judgement is everything, and only years of experience will prevent you from taking wrong options. In the meantime – back your hunches! You learn by trying.

In simple terms, **Flankers** scrummage as hard as Locks! Their role is vital. We also expect the Back Row to be ever alert to control the sideways movement or the wheeling of the scrum. Only movement to our advantage should be permitted. Once the ball is away, the Flankers will be on the move… Add together all their duties and you have, most likely, the busiest men on the field.

***Remember, all players must remain bound in – properly bound – until the ball is out of the scrum.***

A **No.8's** scrummaging duties are less precise – indeed it takes great skill for a No.8 to make maximum contribution to the scrummage effectiveness. *Diagrams F and G on Page 36* give the basic requirement – but it is only experience which teaches a No.8 when to release the ball to his Scrum Half; when to urge his pack to drive forwards taking the ball at his feet or when to attempt a pick-up himself.

It is a fascinating and influential position.

A study of timing. Note that all legs are ready for the drive…

# LINEOUT PLAY

**Including: A) Our Ball, B) Their Ball**

> ❝ *Quality lineout ball gives an excellent platform for attacking rugby. Poor or badly controlled ball is not worth winning… The thrower's accuracy is as vital as the ball winner; the jumper needs expert support players and immediate back up if he is to be successful; it demands concentration and team discipline…*

> *We need to face reality too. The higher up the competitive ladder you climb, the more difficult it becomes to referee the lineout precisely.*
>
> *A good side must quickly assess what a referee will or will not permit and adjust accordingly. As a ball winner, you are going to need great determination and skill; as with the scrummage, this is no place for the faint hearted.* ❞

**MARTIN JOHNSON.**
**Leicester, England and Captain of 1997 British Lions.**

Tim Rodber winning the lineout for England.

# OUR BALL

*With the opposition Threequarter line obliged to be at least 10 metres back from the gain line, our own Backs must be given room to create and manoeuvre; our Forwards must have the option of using their Backs or of keeping the ball up front and driving onwards... In simple language, we MUST control the lineout.*

**Quality Lineout ball** is most important; we want to 'guarantee' ball on our own throw... and get it to our Scrum Half with maximum advantage. (ie. quickly and under control). Frequently, we will make use of the sweeper or second touch man (see below).

*It is, however, essential to realise that the lineout is little short of a battle ground! With two forward packs ready for combat and only a narrow gap of "no-man's-land" between them, it can be pictured as a kind of "trench warfare" with the spoils going to whichever side can win, capture or dominate the trench. Of course you must observe the referee's ruling, but equally you must discover precisely how close to this ruling you can tread without giving away a penalty. You can be quite sure that if your team does not control the "trench zone" – then the opposition will...* **We need to be confident of winning three or four 'safe' throws:**

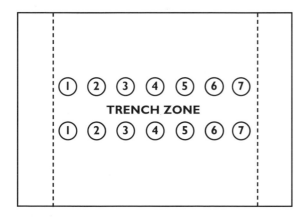

TRENCH ZONE

## i) The fast throw or timed jump.
### (The safest jump)
This is usually a quick throw to No.2 (our front jumper) who gets off the ground before the ball has left the fingertips of the thrower. The jumper must drive forwards and inwards. He must get into the space between the lines. For this throw, you aim to hit the jumper in mid-air. The thrower must practise; the arm should be cocked, ready to fire... Aim for the jumper's face. He will catch it!

## ii) The jump in the middle of the line.
### (Reserve safe catch)
This is another 'safe' jump; an attempt to put the ball in the middle of the Forwards – to be won by our own jumper, secured and then cleared up field. If stolen by the opposition, our players are well spread to defend against attack. This throw is usually a slower, flighted throw, and the classic "salmon's leap" to the very top of the receiver's jump. The "rock and roll jump" – the feint forwards, followed by the move back and up, must be checked with the thrower until perfect...

## iii) Attacking peel from the long throw.
### (The all-out attacking throw)
An exciting attack round the back of the line. Throw to be palmed down by the penultimate man (better than the very back man...) to a fast, powerful player coming round from the front. Sometimes it makes sense to play a strong flanker at Scrum Half for this move; he's ideally placed to run onto the palmed ball...

A two-handed catch at No. 2.

## THE SWEEPER

This man becomes more important if his jumpers or Scrum Half are under severe pressure. (Normally No.1 sweeps back and 6 sweeps forward…) You have to be ready to take the palmed ball or the two-handed catch… You are the link between forwards and the Scrum Half and you will only come in to take the ball if this will help the Scrum Half… (i.e. an extra pair of hands on the ball may slow things down…)

Don't sweep until you have seen that the ball is where you want it. To move and then discover that the plan has gone wrong is a serious mistake…

## THE THROWER

Pin-point accuracy is essential. Use whatever throwing method works best for you. Usually, the job goes to the Hooker – but I prefer to use the best thrower. It takes regular practice – first at a fixed target and then with your jumpers. Communication is vital.

The throw-in is crucial.

## THE JUMPER

Concentration and determination!
- Take your cue from the thrower's arm – not from the ball.
- *"That's my ball!"* attitude is what it's all about. Drive up and at the ball.
- Power and spring can be improved with practice and training. See page 10.
- Success must be judged not on getting a hand onto the ball but on the quality of the ball you deliver to your Scrum Half or support player.
- Two hands are safer than one – but you can reach higher with one. Keep reminding yourself that "bad ball is forbidden…" – especially wet ball near your own line!

### Good advice for jumpers will include:

i) Get in front of your man – even by an inch or two. Use your inside hip.

ii) Develop strong upper body (for wrestling the ball back) as well as a powerful leap.

iii) Never give up competing. Don't just jump and flap your arms…

iv) After a safe catch, begin to turn your body immediately, for delivery to Scrum Half or Sweeper, below waist height, or for a drive through the opposition.

Two hands are safer than one.

## BLOCKING/SUPPORTING

(At the time of going to print, **Lifting** is forbidden in Under 15 Rugby.)

*The referee is expected to penalise contact with your own team or with the opposition – before the ball has been touched by a jumper (i.e. you can't knock the guy over before he's touched the ball!) In practice it's a very difficult zone to get perfect and you need to play to the referee's interpretation...*

*However, all lineout players must understand that no-one comes through our line. There must be no way through the line to get to our Scrum Half.*

Our Ball! Leicester Tigers in action. Martin Johnson with support from Graham Rowntree

The players immediately next to the jumper **must** protect him. They take their timing from the jumper's feet, moving in close, arms binding as tight as is possible to form a total barrier. Here, more than anywhere, we move into the "trench war-fare" zone and this is no place for the faint-hearted... The aim is to leave your jumper free to win and distribute the ball. The blocker behind the jumper should mimic the jumper's body angle. Press right up behind him and keep facing out, to follow play...

Whilst the immediate blockers protect the jumper, the rest of the pack also have work to do. The Scrum Half **must** be protected; a wall of tightly bound bodies "block" the opposition route through the line.

i) Attack the ball.

ii) Compress the line and allow no-one through.

iii) **Those at the ends** have the special duty (shared by the thrower) of ensuring that no-one comes round the line – so face your opponents. Don't turn your back on them...

*This is crucial for the tail-gunner at the back of the lineout; he must protect his Outside Half from the opposition rhinos...*

## SIGNALS

These are the responsibility of the Pack Leader, working with **Thrower** and **Scrum Half**. Every player needs to know and understand the signals or calls...

## SCRUM HALF POSITIONING

Don't get too close to your lineout. (About 5 or 6 feet as a guideline.)

• It is easier to come forwards than to retreat...

• Begin opposite the second or third man in the line – concealing where the ball is going.

# B  THEIR BALL

**Attack their throw!**

• Our Jumper to get in front of their man.
*(It sometimes helps to move one man ahead of their jumper...)*

• Get through or into their line. Our No.6 will attack their tap ball.

• At the back of the line – two players are detailed to think of cover: one checks that the Scrum Half has passed; the other goes for the Outside Half (and then the Centre...) Our Thrower is responsible for getting round the front to put pressure on their Scrum Half.

It is sometimes worth stacking the lineout with all our tall men around their most likely catcher. (ie. all around their No.2 jumper, if we are right on their line...)

If it's foul weather, we emphasise that we do not want any bad ball. We do, however, want them to have bad ball so we all need to compete and hassle them into errors...

## SHORT LINE

Establish your "leaving order" to cope with their short line. Prepare for this and avoid the confusion which your opposition is hoping for.

## DEFENCE AGAINST A PEEL MOVE

**Stop this effective move before it gets going.** The man best placed to put in the first tackle is your back lineout player, who goes forward to block their peeling man.

The England lineout.

# RUCKING AND MAULING

**Including: A) The Ruck, B) The Maul**

 *Get there first! It's our ball and we need to ensure that we keep possession. Secure the ball and look for the back-up players. Whether it's a ruck or a maul, stay on your feet and keep the momentum driving forwards.*

*In today's game, all players must be foragers and support players; everyone must be able to ruck or maul as needed – and we include these practices in every Club session.* 99

**BEN CLARKE.**
**Bedford, England and the British Lions.**

66 *Strong rucking and mauling is an essential ingredient for every top side.*

*We can all learn by studying the best – and, especially for the* **Ruck**, *I point you again and again towards the* **All Blacks** *and their disciplined and awesome standards. Any young player can improve this part of his game by working on fitness and upper body strength – but at the end of the match it is all about determination, teamwork and self belief. The side which dominates here, will usually win.* 99

**TIM RODBER.**
**Northampton Captain, England and the 1997 Lions.**

# A  THE RUCK

Even a light-weight pack can dominate by perfecting the rucking game. Indeed, at schoolboy level, the fast rucking game is very difficult to stop. We look for fast, driving packs who ground the ball when checked and ruck over, giving quick, clean ball for the backs. This puts the opposition back line on the retreat and, hopefully, in disarray; it's very exciting to play and to watch. For a side with superior fitness and gifted support runners it's a fine way to play the game.

*Make sure you really understand this 1–6 practice routine:*

i) Ball-carrier drives into coach/partner.
When he cannot maintain forward momentum, he half turns and forces the ball low and back.
ii) Support players drive in on either side, binding over the back of No.1.
These three players form the Front Row of the ruck.
iii) The next players (4 and 5) drive in binding on 2 and 3 and keep the momentum going.
iv) The ball is placed on the ground (not thrown) – maybe rolled slightly back – and the complete Ruck drives over and upwards, staying on its feet.
v) Any opponents who get into the way are used to bind on.
Make certain that no-one can slip through your Ruck.
vi) This will leave a clean, quick ball for your Scrum Half (or next player).

**"Ball on the deck and drive over."**

The **Ruck.**
Players have bound tight and driven over the ball.

*Remember that forwards can pick up and drive themselves. Or they can pick up and pop a pass to a colleague. Judge the situation. How much space do you have? How close is the defence? Don't become predictable. Don't always just release to the Scrum Half and Threequarters...*

The **All Blacks Rucking** advice...

Any rugby enthusiast will know of the All Blacks and their commitment to a fast, rugged rucking game. Check that you understand the following New Zealand instructions... Is there any difference to the 1-6 practice we've just looked at?

1. **Drive beyond the ball.**
2. **Keep on your feet – keep your opponents on their feet.**
3. **Keep your eyes open.**
4. **Bind.**
5. **Come in low – and up.**
6. **Keep your balance.**
7. **Keep your spine "in line".**

Aim for a 2-3-2 formation with the last man standing off (ready for the ball);
• hook in any other players anywhere near;
• as players arrive they must bend, bind, drive, with legs pumping hard with short strides; drive in hard – **Rucks go forward**;
• keep a strong firm unit – drive over the ball, leaving it alone for the Scrum Half...

# THE MAUL

The purpose of the Maul is to retain the ball in the hands; you then have the option of safety play or an attack. Both need to be understood.

## i – THE DEFENSIVE MAUL

To be set up under pressure.

No 1 – gets hold of the ball.

No 2 – moves in close to support (coming in from behind) and also gets hands on the ball.

No 3 – ensures that 2 has the ball and then concentrates on sealing off/protecting by binding in close and tight.

No 4 – does much the same but on the other side of the ball.

No 5 – can either add weight to the Maul or become the Scrum Half and call for the ball...

Ball in hand – complete control.

## ii – THE ATTACKING OR ROLLING MAUL

Gain full control before beginning the roll.

**Get the ball to the back**, fast; it is then away from the opposition – and your Half Backs have sight of it...

i.e. As for Defensive Maul except that 5 stays close and bound in. Watch an expert team in action and you will realise just how difficult it is to stop. The man at the back can decide whether to release/retain the ball and drive/roll round the edges; break and charge...

**"Get the ball to the back of the bus..."**

# TEST YOUR RUGBY KNOWLEDGE

The four Quiz Sections which follow cover a wide range of Rugby Union knowledge.

They are **not** meant to be easy! Any young player who is able to find the correct answer to a good number of these questions will be heading in the right direction.

Please use the Quiz Section for **discussion** – and try to learn from it…

**QUIZ 1 – Team Selection**

**QUIZ 2 – Mostly about Forward Play**

**QUIZ 3 – Mostly about Threequarters**

**QUIZ 4 – General Rugby knowledge & the laws**

**QUIZ 5 – Name the players**

(Answers and/or page references are included – together with additional notes where helpful…)

Please note – these items are for **discussion** by all players. Sometimes there may be several reasonable answers and in many cases you will need to turn to the indicated page for fuller information.

12 or 13 year-olds are not expected to know all of the answers but they will do well to read, learn and discuss as much as possible. Any young player who is knowledgeable about all **test** sections will be better prepared than many senior club players…

***Tick the boxes only if you understand and can explain or could demonstrate.***

## QUIZ 1

### TEAM SELECTION

Write down the names of your strongest XV.
You may select from any team but you must be able to discuss the qualities required for selection in each position.

15. Full Back:

14. Right Wing:

13. Outside Centre:

12. Inside Centre:

11. Left Wing:

10. Fly Half:

9. Scrum Half:

1. Loose Head Prop:

2. Hooker:

3. Tight Head Prop:

4. Lock:

5. Lock:

6. Blind Side Flanker:

7. Open Side Flanker:

8. Number 8:

Replacements:

| 1 | 2 |
| 3 | 4 |
| 5 | 6 |

Your choice of Captain?

Now compare your team – and the requirements you have for each position – with a knowledgeable friend. If you have the knowledge to deal with this Quiz, you obviously know enough about the game to try Quiz 2…

## QUIZ 2

### Mostly about FORWARD PLAY

1. Explain what you understand by **Quality Possession** from scrum, lineout ❑

2. Consider the difference between the **Loose Head** and the **Tight Head Prop** ❑

3. Explain **Ruck** ❑
and **Maul** ❑

4. The different role of **Openside** and **Blindside Flankers** ❑

5. The **Off Side Law** at
i) Set Scrum ❑
ii) Ruck ❑
iii) Maul ❑
iv) Lineout ❑

6. Can you explain the meaning and importance of the following **Tight Scrummage** terms?
i) "against the head" ❑
ii) "secondary shove" ❑
iii) "binding" ❑
iv) "lock out" ❑

7. Why is **Second/Third Phase ball** so important? ❑

8. Can you explain…
i) Players going "over the top" ❑
ii) "turn-over ball" ❑

9. Explain the **Advantage/Gain Line** at
i) Set Scrum ❑
ii) Line out ❑

10. If the ball is thrown long, over the back of a **Lineout**, when can a player move to catch it? ❑

**(Answers on page 52)**

## QUIZ 3

### Mostly about THREEQUARTERS

1. Give three essential principles of **Back Defence** ❑

2. Explain the difference between **Man for Man** and **Drift Defence** ❑

3. When is it helpful to **Draw your man**? ❑

4. Explain the difference between and when to use the following **Kicks**:
i) Place ❑
ii) Drop ❑
iii) Screw ❑
iv) Grubber ❑
v) Garry Owen ❑

5. Can you demonstrate/explain the following ways of **Beating your man**:
i) Side Step ❑
ii) Change of Pace ❑
iii) Swerve ❑
iv) The Switch or Scissors ❑
v) The Dummy ❑
vi) Introducing the Extra Man ❑

6. Can you explain how the **Back Three** should work together in defence? ❑

7. What happens if a player deliberately throws the ball into touch or off the field of play? ❑

8. What do you understand by a **Smother Tackle**? When might you use it? ❑

9. How, when and where should you **Mark** a ball? ❑

10. Explain the advantages/disadvantages of passing flat or steep ❑

**(Answers on page 52)**

49

# QUIZ 4

## GENERAL RUGBY KNOWLEDGE & THE LAWS.

1. Name the current holders of the Rugby World Cup ❑

When and in what country will the next World Cup be held? ❑

2. In what way does the Under 19 Scrummage Law differ from that of Senior Rugby? ❑

3. Is it a try if:
i) A player touches down **on** (not over) the try line? ❑
ii) A player is held off the ground **over** the try line – and fails to ground the ball? ❑
iii) A player, diving for the try line, touches down before he is tackled into touch, knocking the corner flag over in the process? ❑

4. How many points are scored for
i) a try ❑
ii) a converted try ❑
iii) a drop-goal ❑
iv) a penalty? ❑

5. What should a **Referee** do if:
i) A player's studs are unsafe? ❑
ii) A player has committed a foul, but the opposition seems to have a good chance of scoring a try...? ❑
iii) He thinks that play is dangerous? ❑

6. Give the **definition** of **a Tackle** ❑
What must a tackled player do? ❑

7. After a try has been scored and the conversion has been missed, how should the game be re-started? ❑

8. Do you know why an unconscious person – or a player with a suspected neck or back injury should be moved **only** by a qualified expert...? ❑

9. What is the best way to treat a player who has been **winded**? ❑

10. Where must the ball come out of the **Scrummage**? ❑

**(Answers on page 52)**

# QUIZ 5

### NAME THE PLAYERS

Answers will be found on the page indicated.

**Page 26**

**Page 27**

**Page 40**

**Page 30**

**Page 12**

**Page 30**

**Page 6**

**Page 25**

**Page 2**

**Page 40**

## TEST YOUR RUGBY KNOWLEDGE ANSWERS...

### QUIZ 2 Answers

1) Quality possession: Ball delivered to the Scrum Half under control and as required.
2) Prop Forwards: Ch.8 page 36
3) Ch.10, Page 46. Ruck: ball on the ground. Maul: ball in the hand.
4) Back Row Defence: Ch.7 page 29/30 & 32.
5) Off side Law: Ch.4 page 19.
   i. set scrum: back foot;
   ii. ruck: back foot;
   iii. maul: behind the ball;
   iv. Line out: 10 metres.
6) i. "against the head": scrum ball won by the team not putting in the ball.
   ii. "secondary shove": The first shove "locks" the scrum and secures the ball; the team then regroups before calling for the "secondary drive" – usually with the No 8 controlling the ball with his feet.
   iii. "Binding": gripping another player's shirt or shorts to keep a tight unit.
   iv. "Lock Out": Ch.8 page 36
7) First Phase ball must be won against an organised defence. the defence should be in control.
   Second Phase will usually find your opponents less organised and by Third Phase the advantage may have passed to the attackers.
8) i. "over the top": If a team is likely to win ball on the ground, opponents can prevent the heel by diving over the ball. This is illegal and should be penalised with a penalty kick.
   ii. "Turn-over ball": a player who is tackled will try to ensure that the ball remains on the body side of his own team. A strong tackler can "turn over" the player as he tackles, thus making the ball available for his side.
9) Gain Line/ Tackle Line: diagram page 32.
10) Once the ball has left the fingers of the thrower.

### QUIZ 3 Answers

1) Back Defence: Ch.7 pages 32/33
2) Man for Man is just that; you take your opposite number.
   Drift Defence means that if the opposition move the ball early, it may be possible for your Outside Half to come up on their Inside Centre and "drift" the defence across counter any extra opponents coming into the line.
3) When you want to ensure that he is not going to tackle the man you pass to...
4) See section on Kicking. Ch.4 Esp.16/17
5) Ch.6 pages 27/28.
6) See page 33. Full Back and wingers.
7) A penalty is awarded against him.
8) A tackle which prevents the man from passing the ball.
9) Ch.8 page 15 or see Index "fair catch."
10) Flat passing brings you closer to the gain line – but closer to the defenders. Study Ch.5 page 21.

### QUIZ 4 Answers

1) South Africa. Wales 1999.
2) Under 19 Scrummage may not be driven more than 1.5 m.
3) i. Yes. On the line is a score.
   ii. No. He must ground the ball.
   iii. Yes. He scored before he went into touch.
4) i. 5, ii. 7, iii. 3, iv. 3.
5) i. Send him off to change them.
   ii. Play advantage. If they score – let it stand. If not – give a penalty at the place where the infringement took place. Either way, the referee should let the infringing player know that the offence has been noted.
   iii. Stop the game.
6) See Index. He must immediately release the ball and roll away from it.
7) A drop-out from the half-way line, by the non-scoring side.
8) You'll probably do serious damage if you move him.
9) Let him recover in his own time. Do not attempt to pump him up and down to "help".
10) Anywhere except at either end of the put-in tunnel.

# INDEX OF NAMES AND RUGBY TERMS

*indicates International player in photograph or person contributing to the text

**DROP OUT** Means of restarting play from centre spot or 22m line.

**DUMMY** Pretend…

**EXTRA MAN** (Overlap) "Making an extra man" usually refers to the full-back or a powerful forward coming into the three-quarter line on attack, and thus making his wing an unopposed player *page 28.*

**FAIR CATCH** (or **MARK**) If a player makes a "fair catch" from a kick, a knock-on or a throw forward – within his 22m area – both feet on the ground – calling "Mark!" as he takes the catch, a free kick may be awarded. *Page 15.*

**FITNESS** *chapter 3.*

**GAIN (ADVANTAGE) LINE** An imaginary line drawn across the field through the centre of scrum, line-out, ruck or maul. An attack starts to be effective only when the ball is taken over the gain line. *Page 32.*

**GARRYOWEN** Up-and-Under kick named after the famous Irish club of the same name. High kick ahead designed to give your players time to follow up and cause confusion among defenders waiting for the ball to descend from the skies. The kicker must follow up ahead of his team mates to put them on side. *Page 23.*

**\*GLANVILLE Phil de** *page 2*

**\*GOMARSALL Andy** *page 22 and 24*

**GOAL** Combination of a try (5 points) and a successful conversion (2 points).

**\*GRAYSON Paul** *page viii*

**\*GREENWOOD Richard** *page iv.*

**\*GREENWOOD Will** *page 33*

**\*GUSCOTT Jeremy** *page 8*

**HAND OFF** A way of fending off a would be tackler by pushing him away with the open hand. It may not be a punch…

**HALF TIME** Time between halves. The Coach may come on to the field of play to advise players.

**\*HEALEY Austin** *page 8*

**\*HEALEY Dr. Norman** *page iii.*

**\*JOHNSON Martin** *page ii, 40 and 43*

**KNOCK-ON** The ball bounces forwards off the hand or arm of a player attempting to catch or pick it up. Note the difference with "charge down".

**LATE TACKLE** Tackling a player after he has kicked or passed the ball. If done after a kick, the penalty will be awarded where the ball lands.

**\*LEONARD Jason** *page 30 and 34*

**LIFTING** Gaining greater height for a lineout jumper by hoisting him.

**LINE OF TOUCH** An imaginary line in the field of play, at right angles to the touch line, through the place where the ball is to be thrown in at a lineout.

**LOCK** or **LOCKOUT** "Lock" is another name for "Second Row". Lockout *page 36.*

**MARK** See *FAIR CATCH.* The MARK is the place on the pitch where a free kick or penalty is awarded.

**MAUL** see *page 47*

**MOUTH GUARD** Recommended mouth protection – to be properly fitted by a qualified dentist.

**OFF SIDE** see *page 19*

**\*OJOMOH Steve** *cover picture and page 3*

**"OVER THE TOP"** Preventing fair release of the ball. *Page 18, C(i).*

**PALM BACK** A one handed deflection from the lineout (the inside hand must be used).

**PEELING OFF** A player from the lineout may "peel off" to take the "palm back" from a jumper…

**PENALTY TRY** Awarded when, in the opinion of the referee, a player would have scored if he had not been obstructed by a defender. The conversion kick is taken in front of the posts.

**PROP FORWARDS** Loose Head on the left. Tight Head on the right. *Page 37, 37 and 38.*

**PUSH-OVER TRY** When the attacking pack push the entire scrum back over their opponent's line and drop on the ball.

**QUALITY POSSESSION** Good, clean possession which we can use without being under pressure.

*RAW Michael *page vi*

*REAGAN Mark *page 34*

**REPLACEMENTS** Substitutes allowed to come onto the field to replace an injured player. Six are permitted at U.21 level.

*RICHARDS Dean* *page 1*

*RODBER Tim* *page 30, 40 and 45*

*ROWNTREE Graham *page 34*

*ROWELL Jack *page vii*

**RUCK** *page 46*

**SCISSORS** or **SWITCH MOVE** A pass where the receiver, instead of continuing in the same direction as the receiver, cuts back inside him. (Dummy scissors – the passer pretends to pass to the man on the "scissors".) *page 27.*

*SHAW Simon *page 30*

*SHEASBY Chris *page 19*

**SMOTHER TACKLE** A tackle in which the ball-carrier is not merely stopped but is caught with the ball so that he cannot pass it. *page 27.*

*STIMPSON Tim *page 30*

**STUDS R.F.U.** Safety regulations require studs of at least 10 mm diameter. Referees are expected to inspect studs before a game.

**TACKLE** To be "tackled", a player must be held (by one or more opponents) and **brought to ground** (or the ball into contact with the ground). NB. On one knee, both knees or sitting = tackled *page 13*

**TAP KICK** A tap-kick of only a few inches – made to himself – to restart play.

**TORPEDO (SCREW KICK)** A special spinning type of punt. *page 16*

**TOUCH DOWN** If a defending player grounds the ball in his own in-goal area, this is a touch down, and is followed by a drop out from the 22 line...

**TOUCH IN GOAL** When the ball goes out of play behind the goal-line.

**TRAINING PROGRAMMES** *Ch.3, pages 7–11.*

**TURN OVER BALL** turning the tackled player over the ball so as to leave the ball on your own side.

*UNDERWOOD Tony *page 25*

*UNDERWOOD Rory *page 12*

**WHEELING THE SCRUM** Turning the scrum so that it is sideways across the pitch. Usually a spoiling tactic to prevent opponents winning good ball.

# COACHING RUGBY

## *12-16 Age Group*

To be used in conjunction with

## HEADING FOR THE TOP
### RUGBY FOR AMBITIOUS YOUNG PLAYERS

*All to play for…*

# Contents

*…focus on the next generation*

# The Author's View

" There can be no substitute for teacher quality. A gifted teacher will inspire…"

This section of the book is for those who coach. It examines the game with all parents and teachers who wish to assist in bringing the very best out of ambitious young players. It deals specifically with the 12 to 16 age group, but should be of value to anyone interested in raising standards in junior Rugby Football.

To be used in conjunction with the Young Players' Book **Heading for the Top**

*Our aim, here, in* "**Coaching Rugby – 12 to 16 Group**", *is to focus on the next generation of young enthusiasts; young players who have already been introduced to the game but who now look for guidance and positive motivation if they are to choose Rugby as their main sport in the years ahead…*

*With the rapid growth of the game in recent years, there has been no shortage of encouragement and advice for senior players. The Over 16 Group is well represented right through to a highly competitive International side. So, too, is the MINI Group (the U.11 youngsters) for whom the RFU has produced an excellent series of colour pamphlets. For young players, perhaps the best known and most comprehensive introduction to the game is the RFU's own* "**Even Better Rugby**", *which teaches the game from absolute beginnings to the 7–11 group.*

**Coaching Rugby** *is also firmly intended as a coaching challenge; to stimulate debate; to stir a little adrenalin; to encourage our coaches to learn from the most positive innovations introduced by Rugby League; to seek a share of the higher levels of vision and ambition which at present come mainly from the southern hemisphere and which, with the right preparation, can be reached by our own youngsters.*

*Throughout the rugby world, there will be many teachers and coaches who recognise the need for discussions, specific to this age. Anyone who has worked with the 12 to 16 Group will be aware not only of the exciting potential but also of the complexities which sometimes accompany adolescence. Coaches will be interested to compare ideas and evolving playing patterns, and to examine teaching methods. Hopefully, too, they may be willing to contribute to further understanding of how best to guide young players of the future.*

*The Players' Book. –* **Heading for the Top** *– is written for young people. To capture attention, I make use of photographs and advice from a number of highly experienced Internationals and Coaches; I also use action shots of young players to illustrate many of the skills. We offer a balance of encouragement, challenge and instruction – but much more than that, we try to show that this is a sport which is worthy of support and loyalty.*

# *The Changing Game*

Rugby Union continues to grow rapidly. Both on and off the field we see a rapidly changing game and, as coaches, we must be aware not only of these changes but of how they may influence the junior game.

Here, I select several areas for debate…

## 1) What lessons can be learned from the playing success of the top international nations?

In our own country and in our own special conditions, we have players who can match any in the world. In more general terms, and at international level in particular, we would be foolish to ignore the obvious fact that southern hemisphere nations are producing the more successful sides. We need to be ready to re-examine levels of fitness, of maturity, of attitude – to analyse what is best in the game and, where suitable, to include it in our own junior programmes.

*It is our task to note the alterations in the adult game and try to steer a positive line which will be of help to our young players. In playing terms, we applaud teams trying to develop the exciting, athletic game of running and handling. By watching and imitating, our young players can only be encouraged to raise skill levels, but, realistically, how many coaches have access to a full XV of pace, power, skill and determination? What applies to the adult professional game may not always be suited to the Under 16 players – and it is our intention to keep alert to such differences.*

## 2) Improvements in fitness levels, combined with a number of law changes, have brought about a different and more exciting style of international play.

No longer is it a game for rigid set positions and isolated roles; it is becoming faster and more dynamic – a game of exciting continuity. Today's more enterprising coaches involve the whole team wherever possible.

## 3) Additional fitness requirements can pose difficulties.

As Junior age-group coaches, we recognise the need for our pupils to enjoy other activities – and indeed other sports; we do not demand total dedication to the game and we run into difficulties if we impose too rigid a regime. However, without increasing fitness demands, we will not achieve the higher standards which make the modern game worth playing. We must devise a balance.

In my opinion, though, we can raise standards, without losing the fun of it all and becoming too solemn…

Coaches must make fitness work enjoyable – especially when dealing with young enthusiasts. I hope you will study the chapter on **Fitness and Safety** (page 69) – and draw your own conclusions.

## 4) The challenge of "Skills for all" can also pose difficulties.

The theory is sound of course; we wish all our players to run like gazelles, show handling dexterity and master numerous skills from virtually every position… The reality is different: we have youngsters of contrasting size, shape and commitment. We still applaud the **Skills for all** ideal and will encourage all our players to practise many skills – basing our reasoning on the understanding that a youngster's playing position may alter over the years ahead. The reality of course is that, like it or not, most of us will be forced to include in our team several "less gifted" players – players who will need to be coached to "do the job" to the best of their ability. They will struggle, at this age certainly, to be top-line players and, to some extent, will be handicapped by the demands of the new, faster, multi-skilled game. We need to keep a special eye on these youngsters in our changing game; some of them may well be late developers and valuable club players in years to come. We must surely keep a place for them.

**5) We also take note of the most recent safety guidelines (see chapter 5).**

**6) Essentially though, the playing format of junior rugby has not altered greatly.**

We still aim to secure the ball, from set scrum or lineout (phase 1); then, pull apart the opposition defence lines by making a break or by setting up ruck or maul (phase 2); then, attack in unprotected areas using phase 3 or even phase 4 ball. Junior age group rugby has always been like this – whatever the complications of the senior game.

In U.16 rugby, we continue to look for a test of handling, pressure, support and organisation – but in today's game we expect players to be more aware of just how they can influence the game by adding support play to their recognised role. Because of improved fitness levels, we now think in terms of introducing extra players into hitherto unexpected parts of the field.

To aid our junior game, I would like to see a further tightening of the **OFF-SIDE LAW**. Referees must be encouraged to penalise the loiterers and the fringe players who continue to stand in the way of an expansive game. Not only is this a curse of international matches, it takes much of the movement away from the junior game.

**7) A game for girls?**

Here, too, there has been considerable change which needs careful attention. There is increasing interest in the female game and barriers are coming down all over the globe. What is required is for the RFUW to benefit from lessons learned by the RFU and to be assisted in these important early years. Just as the 12 to 16 Boys group needs to be considered as a specific Group, so too we will need to give special attention to the requirements of the girls. The skills material for ambitious young players can be for male or female and holds good for the 12 to 16 group.

# THREE

# Coaching Objectives

We know that we were fortunate if we came under the influence of a really outstanding coach or teacher – particularly at an age when lasting impressions were made. I rate the 12 to 16 age-group coaching experience as perhaps the most influential… Here, I list a few of my own Coaching Objectives.

## SPARKLE

The best coaches are facilitators – not martinets. They aim to ignite talent. They search for a balance which embraces ambition and vision; "fire in the belly" as well as generous sportsmanship. And, where they find it, they cultivate exuberance and flair.

## ATTITUDE

Young players like to know precisely where they stand – and what you, the coach, stand for… The coach's attitude sets the tone for all players to follow – especially influential on a young captain. How well your players react in a tight situation, to success or failure, is greatly down to you…

## FITNESS

Youngsters deserve the chance to become really fit – well prepared in body and mind. Your physical and mental training programmes can help them to reach into exciting new territory and, clearly, a team which is fitter than its opponents, takes an immediate advantage.

Those coaches involved with the higher levels of intensive training must be mindful not only of the benefits of correct exercise, but also of areas which can over-stress the growing frame. (Section 5, page 69)

## EXPERIENCE

The sensitive coach has a positive role to play in steering young players along the way. Competitive sport tends to bring more than its share of contact with those two imposters "triumph" and "disaster" and few are better positioned than the coach to listen and to advise.

## TECHNIQUE

Size and strength are important factors but, as the level rises, technique also becomes essential. "Start them young and start them right!" is a sound coaching philosophy. Where possible, show them the very best players in action (or on video) and let them imitate…

## YEARLY ASSESSMENTS

Just as you expect to assess the players' progress so you need to check your own. Rugby is a changing game and coaches need to be clear about their thinking. I won't dwell on such an obvious point except to emphasise the value and enjoyment of attending a refresher course…

## SAFETY

Safety has to be paramount and you need to know what you are talking about. In today's climate, a coach must be knowledgeable about basic First Aid and about how to deal with the specific risk areas of the game (page 73). In a tough, contact sport like ours there must be knocks and bruises and no serious minded rugby critic will object to these. Foul or deliberately dangerous play or behaviour needs rooting out at the youngster level.

## PRIORITIES

We benefit by setting out our priorities. I've known too many coaches become fanatical about their coaching, to the detriment of family and friends. And yet it takes real dedication to reach the higher levels. There needs to be a balance, and experience suggests that it helps to write down and discuss our coaching priorities.

## OPPORTUNITIES

Looking back, as only an experienced coach is able to do, I see this as a key heading. To today's coaches and players I say simply, "Grasp every opportunity as if it is special. Do it while you can."

## RESPONSIBILITY

*And here I must add "risk factor". Media attention has been increasingly drawn towards the referee/teacher/pupil responsibility zones. If a serious accident occurs, it is not enough nowadays to claim that you did not understand your role. You need to look carefully at Rules, Regulations and The Law – and only a fool will avoid this extremely serious aspect of our work with young people.*

Also, under **Responsibility**, we need to look carefully at what can be asked of young players. Not only do they respond to being invited to take on special duties – both on and off the field. – they positively thrive on such trust. (Looking after visitors, the referee or equipment; even looking after a less experienced colleague…). One tends to think only of the Captain's role, but every player should be encouraged to help to promote the game…

## TEACHING, QUALITY AND VISION

There can be no substitute for teacher quality. A gifted teacher will inspire – will communicate his or her belief in the special qualities of the pupils – and remarkable results can be achieved. At the end of the day, however, a young player will achieve only that which he believes is possible. Thus, since many of us under-estimate our own potential, it requires skill and expert guidance to bring out the best in others…

The satisfaction of coaching this age-group lies not solely in producing a winning team, but in helping a young side to play to its full potential. We glean huge pleasure from watching a talented XV demonstrate its skill, but reward too from encouraging a side of no-hopers to perform above their expectations. Once in a while, if we are fortunate, we find ourselves in charge of an outstanding group of exciting promise…

It is important, also, to stress the need for vision – for an ability to assess what is truly best for our young players in a rapidly developing scene. Few sports in recent years, have encountered more dramatic changes than Rugby Union and we need to keep a close eye on the way forward…

# Teaching Guidelines

The Under 16 game... Rugby Football coaching technique is a constantly evolving challenge. I know of not one single successful coach who is complacent about his knowledge and expertise in a changing game. Every season brings with it new challenges – new ideas on how to approach old problems and new attempts by the legislators to improve the game... The following **Teaching Guidelines** illustrate some of my own observations in Under 16 Rugby; I list these few points because they have been helpful to me...

### 1) Offer your Pupils a Genuine Challenge

We must recognise that youngsters constantly need to be challenged – to achieve, to succeed, to feel good. Set them high standards which will stretch them enough to demand their concentrated effort and show them that you are interested... Records and display boards can provide the evidence of well earned success.

### 2) Youngsters Learn Best from Watching and Imitating

Use of a recent video or a live demonstration makes a far clearer imprint than any talk. Today's technology, combined with our own coaching knowledge, allows us to show the very best action shots for young players to imitate. Teach what to watch for and then help by providing the appropriate skills practice at the next session.

### 3) Teach in a Defined Area

Far too much teaching time is wasted by using the entire playing area.

Concentrate skills coaching into defined areas – Grids or the 22 – where every player can be seen and coached. I like to use the Sports Hall or tarmac surface to practise many of the skills, using the small area to concentrate attention.

### 4) "Simple to Complex; Individual to Unit"

Even the very best players need to build up a handling/running confidence rhythm – every time.

### 5) Work with Discipline and Control

Rugby is a hard enough game without adding confusion. Young players respect the right application of discipline and will work much better once they are clear about the control limits. There is no excuse for the undisciplined session – but that certainly does not prohibit laughter...

### 6) Variety and Repetition

Keep things moving. Stimulate your teaching by introducing variety but repeat the sections which matter most...

### 7) Encouragement and Humour, not Sarcasm

This needs little clarification but how easily we all fall into the trap...

Most young boys enjoy being pushed hard and being discouraged from fussiness or softness, so long as this is mixed with good humour and high standards. Areas such as "language", promptness, kit and so on must be part of what the boys understand by "standards". No boy respects a sadist – or a whimp!

### 8) Study the Fitness Chart and Safety Section

Few areas of our game are altering more quickly.(Section 5, page 69.)

Young people will look to you for guidance.

### 9) We are Teaching Under 16 Individuals

What suits the adults may not necessarily fit well into the young player's programme. Some skills and tactics which are shown on the International scene are certainly not suitable for the Junior game. Some objectives may be different. Most important of all, youngsters need to be inspired in a way which senior players may have forgotten...

### 10) Self Assessment

I constantly return to this need for self assessment... Try doing the same tests that you so often give to the youngsters. The Quiz questions? The Fitness tests ?

If you find room for improvement – the point is made...

### 11) And perhaps it will help to study again the **Confidence Chart**...

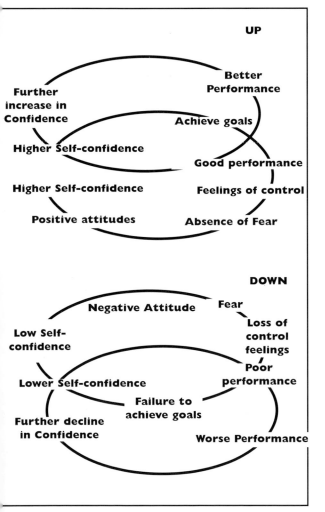

Eventually, you have to put your coaching to the test – and this is where you use a simple **Game Plan**. The more sophisticated the players, the more detailed can be the plan. All your players should have a clear idea of what is likely to happen given a certain situation... I try to keep it as simple as possible.

I use a wall chart or a board and talk through "**ATTACK**" and "**DEFENCE**" in each of three areas: i. Our 22; ii. Mid-field and iii. Their 22. For each area I look at "**scrum ball**" (ours/theirs); "**lineout ball**" and "**loose or penalty ball**". Once we have discussed the options, we take them onto the playing area and go through them again. Far from destroying the "flair" player, this additional understanding encourages confidence.

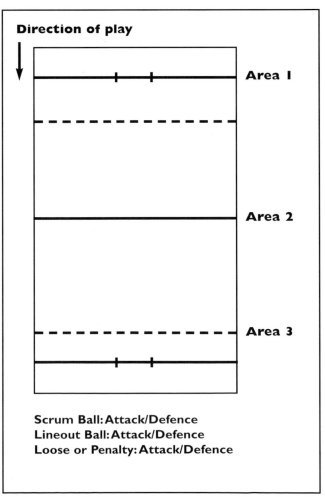

Scrum Ball: Attack/Defence
Lineout Ball: Attack/Defence
Loose or Penalty: Attack/Defence

### 12) The Action Plan and the Game Plan

Every Coach needs an **Action Plan** – a building plan which takes him step by step along the way. It needs little elaboration – but even with young players I have found that it helps to share the planning...

### 13) Match Analysis

Every Coach will have his own method of analysis – of pinning what actually happened in a game. In an action-packed contest, not even the best organised coach can watch everything and this is where knowledgeable parents or colleagues can be of enormous help. Keep their "tasks" simple and insist on the "helpers" reporting back to you and not to the players!

*What happened in the lineouts? Our ball/their ball?*
*How did we use Loose ball? Penalties? &c.*

Even if you decide to back your own judgement, it often helps to have a second opinion…

|  | 50% Line | |
|---|---|---|
| **Ball won, Loose** | | |
| **Ball won, Set** | | |
| **Lineouts won** | | |
| **Scrums won** | | |
| **Possession** | | |
| **Territory** | | |
| **Penalties** | | |
| | **Team A** | **Team B** |

**Additional notes for future reference:**

# Fitness & Safety Notes

The demands of a vigorous contact sport are many but, so long as they fall within the Laws of the Game, they are accepted by players and coaches. In this Chapter, we take for granted standard safety areas (stud checks before all games; padded posts; flexible corner flags; the crack down on unsafe play and behaviour). There remain, however, a number of coaching/teaching points which I believe deserve our further attention...

**It is not always helpful to raise all these issues with the young players themselves, but any serious minded coach will wish to share these areas of concern with others in similar situations...**

In this section, I include:-

**A) Safety in Under 16 Rugby
B) Fitness Training for this Age-group
C) Concern Areas or Awkward Playing Situations
D) Injuries – A Coach's Role
E) Additional Notes
F) Insurance Cover**

## A) SAFETY IN UNDER 16 RUGBY...?

Parents who watch the juddering tackles, the writhing mauls and the flailing fists of much top level rugby are likely to question the wisdom of encouraging their child to participate in such a game. As Coaches, we must recognise their right to question the problem areas; we must find time to reassure them that their youngster is in the hands of a capable coach.

It is quite easy to produce statistics to support almost anything we want to believe. True: rugby has its share of injuries – but fewer than many other activities. True: there are risks in any contact sport. True: youngsters enjoy the challenge and the rough and tumble of rugby. And, True: rugby is not for everyone.

As Coaches we must recognise the sensitive areas

(see page 73) prepare players to deal with them and insist on the highest standards of safety and common sense at all times. We make no attempt to pretend that there is no element of risk – only that the risk is calculated and that preparations are of a high standard and judged to be acceptable...

There is, of course, a serious lobby of opinion which would arrange all junior rugby on a "weight" basis – rather than by age. This solves certain problems but introduces others and neither arrangement is perfect. It remains part of the coach's domain to determine how best to include the "outstanding" youngster without causing complications.

Safety becomes a larger problem as the more serious competitive element creeps in. At the lower levels there is less at stake; a big, aggressive opponent can be 'permitted' a free gallop to the line – but once tournament medals or emotional spectators become involved the defending players feel honour-bound to attempt the tackle... So, where lies the solution? Do we hold back the mature boy? Do we push him up a level so that he is playing with his weight? Indeed, do we recognise that often the 'heavy' boy is short of muscle and will be badly at risk wherever we place him?

*Anyone who is able to produce a fool-proof answer is likely to be exposing his own lack of experience, the only certainty is that every difficult case must be treated on merit – and with great care.*

**"Safe Practice in Physical Education"**

One of the most helpful and up-to-date books on the subject of Safety in Sport is "**Safe Practice in Physical Education**" – produced for BAALPE by White Line Press, Bradford. This looks at the entire range of games and sports for young people and makes important reading for anyone involved in the teaching or coaching of sport.

I quote just one section from their Introduction:

*"The purpose of this book is to advise on safe practice across the range of activities regularly included in PE, and where necessary to interpret statutory and case law, so that teachers can approach their daily work with confidence, learning from the accumulated wisdom of more experienced colleagues."*

## B) FITNESS TRAINING FOR THIS AGE GROUP

*One key reason for this Chapter is to question generalities.*

Player Chapter 3 (Are You Fit to Play Rugby?) illustrates how individual athletes can be encouraged to help themselves. A player who is fitter than an opponent takes an immediate advantage. Correct fitness training cuts down the injury rate and allows skilful performance for longer periods. QED – we must ensure that our players are super fit. However…

**What applies to adult players will not always suit youngsters.**

Aware of the advantages which come with increasing fitness, we need to look sensibly at how we introduce the area of **Intensive Training**… Whilst improving our programmes, we need to become far more sensitive to the increase in "over-use" injuries among many of our most promising young athletes…

*For several years now there has been growing concern amongst coaches, parents and members of the medical profession regarding the effects of too much intensive training on this age group. Those ambitious adults who call for serious training and competition to begin before puber-*

*ty must pause for thought. Certainly, we want our young players to become extremely fit but not at any price. We need to ask ourselves if we can achieve this objective without introducing unnecessary strains and stresses in these early years? There is everything to gain from a sharp, demanding fitness session so long as ample recovery time is provided, any concern should lie with programmes involving the wear and tear of "over-use" and repetitive slog.*

**Thus a crucial question for any Coach must be: "How hard should I drive young players?"**

In the intensity of a hard fought match, we often see young players pushing themselves to new limits. They run faster, cover wider, tackle harder and drive themselves far beyond anything with which we challenged them in the practice session. Clearly, this is the level at which we should be aiming on the training grounds; intensive bursts of play, followed by rest. We have rightly become conditioned to err on the side of safety and to back off before a youngster becomes over-tired or discouraged, but so long as rest is part of the recommended programme, and so long as we know our players' limitations, we can safely drive quite hard. To prepare young players properly for competitive action, we should help them to feel comfortable with the paces and pressures of match conditions – and that means intensive practice sessions.

No two youngsters require precisely the same programme. For convenience, we include them all in group sessions, but the Coach will be mindful of many physical and indeed psychological differences. Some 14 year olds have the physical development of adults and you, the Coach, have the complicated task of balancing their requirements with those of less mature colleagues. Anyone who has worked for long with this age group will recognise the dilemma. Clearly, we must avoid too many generalities and treat each individual case on its merits…

**As a firm guide line, for this level, I prefer coaches to give skill coaching and enjoyment a higher priority than merely winning matches.** The more competitive youngsters are not going to appreciate such an observation but this makes it all the more essential that the Coach can see further than the immediate competition…

Training sessions can be intensive and enjoyable. In my experience, the most positive results for this age come from a well prepared short session – usually including plenty of games or contests – leaving time at the end for chatter and laughter.

## THE CONTENT OF A TRAINING SESSION…

"**Are You Fit To Play Rugby?**" (Player Chapter 3) provides common sense answers to a number of the questions which young players tend to ask… Included for them is a short item on **Individual Training**.

Guidelines include the key sections:

**Endurance**

**Flexibility**

**Speed**

With special reference to this age-group's fitness needs.

**Power Training** (*the combined result of strength and speed*) is looked at separately, and with some care. Intensive Power Training is regarded as standard for the adult player but is listed by experts as unwise for the growing youngster. Any ambitious young player will demand an explanation…

*Medical experts discourage too much attention to strength training until the frame is ready. Any sort of heavy weight training is frowned upon at this age – until the bones have hardened or developed, usually around the age of 16 or 17 years of age. Essentially, what needs to be explained to our young enthusiasts is that short, sharp power sessions of any form of carefully graded training are perfectly acceptable – even for a growing youngster, but OVERLOAD SESSIONS where a set of muscles is given repeat maximum treatment are not recommended.*

## MENTAL PREPARATION

*I include a section on Mental Preparation here because, used sensibly, it can be a powerful aid to both Fitness and Safety. Youngsters will want more information…*

One has only to observe the immediate improvement in Fitness Test results if a brief period of concentration, or mental preparation, is permitted before testing begins.

It is impossible to determine, precisely, where physical fitness ends and mental fitness starts. It is difficult to state with any certainty the influence which a player's physical state has upon his mental state – or vice versa – but the two are closely inter-related.

It is, however, relevant here to observe how much more frequently points are scored during the final period of a contest, when fitness levels and concentration are most stretched. In purely competitive terms, there is clear advantage for a team mentally alerted to raise its game in the 'final' period.

One does not wish to over-pressurise this young age-group, but even young players need to be aware of the benefits induced by correct mental preparation. It makes good sense to talk with them about "positive thinking", about "stress" or "pressure management" and teach them to visualise match situations before they arise. "Be in control under pressure" is a sensible line to aim for.

## FITNESS AND SKILL TESTS.
### (See pages 10 to 11 in the Player's book)

Young players – indeed players of every age – like to see a record of improvement. I constantly challenge players with tests of fitness and/or skill – as an additional spur to training.

Wherever possible I make use of competitions and games taken from other sports. The "Keep the ball off the ground" skill of all footballers; various partner heading contests; basketball handling, dribbling or shooting skills. They all add variety and enjoyment and broaden the skill base. Above all they are fun.

Name _____     Sport _____

Position (if relevant) _____

**Fitness requirement to compete at top levels**

Speed ☐ ☐                    Endurance ☐ ☐

Mobility ☐ ☐                  Strength ☐ ☐

Agility ☐ ☐

**Mental Requirements**

Concentration ☐ ☐            Mental toughness ☐ ☐

Alertness ☐ ☐                Relaxation ☐ ☐

'Switch on/switch off' ☐ ☐   Ambition ☐ ☐
(eg several matches/day/
periods of inactivity etc)

**Other Key Factors:**

Skill ☐ ☐                    Tactical awareness ☐ ☐

Experience ☐ ☐              Knowledge ☐ ☐

*In the first box, rate, on a scale of 1 to 5, how important these factors are to compete at the highest levels in your sport.*

*In the second box, rate yourself on a scale of 1 to 5 in this factor:*

1 = Not important at all
2 = Of some value but other things mean
    much more
3 = Quite important
4 = Very important
5 = As important as anything

1 = I am very weak in this area
2 = I am not so good in this area
3 = Not particularly strong or weak
4 = It is an area which I rate quite highly
5 = It is my strong point

## C) CONCERN AREAS AND AWKWARD PLAYING SITUATIONS

*Size, shape and strength vary so much at this age that certain playing situations can present awkward body positions which need special care.*

### i) The Tackle

Basic tackling is covered in Player Chapter 4 and in most coaching books. There will always be knocks and bruises but seldom danger. The one tackle which demands extra attention is the **Head on Tackle**. The risk involves the young player, often a Centre Threequarter, who assumes that his job is to perform a 'crash tackle' on an opponent coming straight at him; it is very difficult to make that into a safe exercise for an immature youngster. I prefer to encourage a player to 'let the opponent come'; to take him 'from the side' and to use the opponent's momentum to bring him down. As the instruction emphasises (For the more advanced tackler p.13) it is a low drive which lifts into the tackle, and turns to land on top of the opponent. Taught first of all on thick matting in the gym, this becomes a safe and satisfying method of defence.

The other tackle note to mention here involves the **Tackle Bag Practice** area. It is sensible to restrict the run-up for the tackler. Too often one sees the enthusiastic tackler working up a head of steam, hitting a free-standing bag hard, following the instruction to "Hang on!" while the rest of the body flies onwards, often into neck or spine twisting difficulty. Three or four paces is a much safer run-up distance...

### ii) The Front Row and the Second Row in the Scrummage.

We are all aware of the over-weight boy who gets "hidden" in the front row, and of the taller, lankier athlete whose body shape doesn't fit easily into the scrum.

One helpful way round most of these difficulties is to play a lot of 3 v 3 scrums, certainly at the start of the season. This way you build up the necessary muscles and specific fitness and you cut down, significantly, the injury risk. Once you introduce your Second Row, your problems multiply. It stands to reason that early teaching is best done on a scrummage machine, where regular attention can be paid to correct binding, foot work and body angles. I know of coaches who play early season games without the Flankers and this seems to keep the game flowing better...

Law 20. Clause 2. LAWS OF THE GAME for U.19 GROUP reads:

"...In the interests of safety, each front row should engage in the sequence of crouch, then pause, and only engage on the call 'engage' given by the referee..."

Any experienced Prop forward will tell you how easy it is to collapse a scrum without being caught. Early coaching must teach the foolishness of such action.

### iii) Loose Play

Only experience can tell a coach or referee when to stop loose play. There are more injuries in the loose than are caused by tackling and scrummaging put together – and it's all because the body lines become disorganised. Once a head has gone "down" or a body has twisted, a dangerous situation has occurred and wise refereeing is essential. The cry of "Stay on your feet!" makes good sense from every angle.

Talk to the boys all the time. Tell them what you want. Maintain a flow of advice and instruction...

## D) INJURIES – A COACH'S ROLE?

Experienced coaches will immediately recognise a difficult section of "no man's land". Injured players must be the doctor's territory but every coach will be called upon to advise on or to deal with minor injuries when no medical expertise is on the spot... "Coaching Objectives" (page 64) correctly advises caution – but there are a number of pointers to add:

### 1. Prevention is better than cure.

Sports safety awareness is improving quickly now but many accidents remain avoidable. We need not spend time, here, re-enforcing the obvious (*stud checks, dangerous equipment or play, insurance cover, vehicle access to the playing area, &c.*) It must be the responsibility of one senior official to make a regular safety check. His or hers should be a voice with authority and safety must be paramount.

### 2. The Touch-line doctor?

As a referee or a coach, in a match or in a practice, you must be prepared for any eventuality. It is not realistic to insist on a touch-line doctor at all times but, failing that, you must be absolutely confident that you have a sound back-up team in place – even at practice sessions. It is incredible how often the junior sides are inadequately covered and, in today's climate of claim and counter claim, neither you nor your Club can afford to take a chance.

### 3. Help from the Coach?

**i) Psychological aspects** – The experienced coach who knows his job will make the injury problem less traumatic. There will always be the border-line decision regarding the "injured" who merely needs encouragement to get up and play on – and the "genuine" case who needs attention. If you "err on the side of safety" you will not go wrong.

**ii) Rehabilitation** – This is a much neglected area in which a helpful coach can play a most important part. It is for the doctor to recommend that rehabilitation exercising should begin and, clearly, the services of a trained physio become most helpful. However, a coach who takes the trouble to be guided by a fully qualified physiotherapist can often cut down on wasted time and can frequently build up a valuable bond of confidence with the injured player. Too often, at all levels, we see the injured person completely ignored while injured or ill and then, when needed by the team, thrown back into a full game situation. Rehabilitation implies graded progressions back towards full fitness. It is part of a coach's role to understand this important subject and to be able to help.

### E) ADDITIONAL NOTES

**i) Psyching Up** – Any coach will be aware that he can raise his teams' performance, at least for a while, with a spell of powerful psyching up. Unscrupulous coaches readily overuse such tactics and the game becomes too serious. The old adage: "It's not a matter of life and death; it's far more important!" easily springs to mind. It is easy to refer you back to the section on **Coaching Objectives** but it remains an area for care…

**ii) Parents** – Most parents are an important support and a real tonic for the coach during a long season. Some need to be gently but firmly dissuaded from over-zealous support, or barracking of the referee or opposition. Beware of those vicariously re-living their youth!

**iii) Coaching from the Touchline** – Should be banned! It is unhelpful in every way – not least in its undermining of the captain and the inhibition of the boys' capacity to make their own decisions.

**iv) Mouth Guards** – In spite of the improvements made with the do-it-yourself mouthguard, I strongly advise youngsters to get properly fitted protection. There is no comparison and the extra money is worth spending…

**v) Ear Tape** – Many top players are seen to use strips of adhesive tape to protect their ears. They wouldn't use tape unless this did in fact help them… On the down side, tape can cut and rip the skin and, with younger players, I much prefer to encourage the use of proper head guards.

### F) INSURANCE COVER

Schools and Clubs, affiliated to the RFU, must have block insurance for all Members – but it is sensible to check precisely what that 'cover' includes. It is important, for example, to ensure that 'member cover' is extended to include others who occasionally take part – players, coaches or helpers. It is also essential to insist that anyone 'helping' to transport young players to away matches should have the appropriate motor insurance cover. The onus is on the School or the Club to make clear what cover is required but, as any sports person will know, there are still far too many grey areas… Any person who regularly works with young people must realise that insurance cover is no longer a matter to treat casually.

# Rugby Union Skills

This section adds **Coaching Notes** to the **Young Player Chapters** in "**Heading for the Top**".

## 1. RUGBY SKILLS FOR ALL PLAYERS (*page 12*)

*Ambitious young players should be encouraged to master a wide variety of skills and to gain experience in a number of alternative positions.*

*With increasing intensity in School and Club competitions, the demand for "results" is ever with us. There is a temptation to finalise positions and to specialise on positional skills as soon as possible. "Skills for All" implies that in the early years, players will benefit from being given as broad a skill base as time will permit. The wise coach will be constantly weighing requirements – mindful of the young player's needs and of the physical changes which he may encounter over the coming years...*

*I believe, also, as part of the educational progression, in sharing certain responsibility with the players. I like to discuss with them the ACTION PLAN or THE GAME PLAN – the plan which Coach and Captain consider to make the best use of the available players in training or in the actual matches. Young players respond to sensible discussions and a degree of shared responsibility – even if, at the final count, the buck stops with the coach...*

## 2. TACKLING (*page 13*)

Please note the additional section on The Head on Tackle in the Fitness and Safety chapter, page 73.

## 3. THE HIGH BALL (*page 14*)

The Defensive Fall (p.15). Excellent lead in to the Defensive Maul. Small group coaching is essential.

## 4. TOUCH RUGBY LEAGUE (*page 16*)

Regular practice of Touch Rugby or Sevens, in a restricted area, can bring rapid improvement of many skills. I like to use it as an early season appetiser – aware of the fact that every individual can immediately be active and improving skills. I like to "plan" the unsupervised non-tackling sessions which enthusiastic youngsters will play in their spare time. I anticipate their game; go over the essential rules; appoint the "referee" and detail the playing area. I encourage youngsters to play Touch in small groups while I am concentrating on another group on a different part of the field. Clearly, there can be no contact play unless an adult referee is in charge.

*I prefer the League style re-start after a break-down. The "touched" man must stop and play the ball back between his legs. The next player must pass immediately and the game is not held up...*
*(I also use this League re-start for an occasional tackling practice game – carefully refereed; it involves lots of close quarter work, making tackling much safer and more rewarding.)*

## 5. KICKING SKILLS (*page 16*)

However strongly you advocate a "running" game, most youngsters will wish to try their luck at Kicking – so, as a compromise, I introduce a Kicking lesson at this early stage. I am aware that

only a few will specialise but by teaching the basics I hope to avoid the ineffective kick-about which occupies so much valuable time.
Good kicking does require individual specialist attention. I like to introduce the different styles and give plenty of time for experiment on their own.

It makes sense to set achievable progressions and give instructions to tick off as each target is reached. Eventually, I set aside specialist clinic time for those who need it.

## 6. PENALTY LAWS (page 18)

Teach them early; you can't expect a high standard until they understand the rules of the game...

In encouraging young players to persevere with a wide, attacking game, one has to be aware that the OFF SIDE Law must be carefully observed. At present, systematic spoiling and laying up on (or over) the off-side line militates against sides trying to play an attacking game. The 3 point penalty kick at goal may need changing.

## 7. THE HALF BACKS (page 20)

*I regard the Half Back combination as the key link in Junior Rugby. Because of this I spend a few moments at the start of almost every session just ensuring the quality of this vital pair...*

In recent years, there has been a deal of talk about **alignment** – to **stand steep or flat**. Outside Halves tend to be labelled as `runners', `passers' or `kickers'.

Clearly, we need a combination of all three, to be used as required. Much depends on our opposition and the referees interpretation of the Off-side Law (see above). If the opposition defence is well back, then our backs can be flattish and close to the gain line (see diagram: p.21)

What is crucial, in attack, is to ensure that our Outside Half "occupies"or "fixes" the first defender – usually the Open-side Flanker – thus giving the wider strike runners space and decision time...

**Reminders for the Half Backs...**
Key to success: "Be comfortable at all times..."
*i) Establish length of SH pass and always work*

*to be one metre inside this.*
*ii) SH puts the ball where the OH dictates.*
*iii) OH never moves (unless sweeping blind or changing direction of play...) until the ball has left the SH's hands.*
*iv) OH runs as straight as is comfortable for him.*

## 8. THE XV in ATTACK (page 25)

In days gone by, this would have been headed "Threequarters in Attack". Now, however, we think in terms of the entire team...

*"Attack" without a sound base is fairly pointless. What we want from this chapter is an attitude which will always be alert to the split second when "attack" can become a reality. The positive attitude which is ready to take advantage of the opponent's moment of weakness or relaxation; the attitude which allows the complete XV to be thinking of counter-attack rather than total defence. The determination to get into position – ready to attack again and again – to "dare to try it" – even if we sometimes fail...*

**With our top players, we need to teach:**
i) the ability to pass flat and with confidence while running at the defence.
ii) the ability to hold a short pass fractionally in the air for a close runner.
iii) the ability to fire a long ball at a distant space for a straight or angled runner.
iv) the discipline and confidence to run at 75 % speed to draw defenders.
v) the control to use one of the following options:
    pass the ball close
    pass the ball wide
    kick
    move the ball early
    hit the tackle and present the ball.

## 9. THE TEAM IN DEFENCE (page 31)

*All players must understand the team's defensive strategy. I deal with this as a very early priority and it seems to help greatly with confidence. The players need to know their role.*

With young players, I favour a simple Man for Man understanding – individual players are detailed to "Take your own man". More skillful youngsters may be able to master a more effcient

Drift Defence. (The Outside Half taking the opposing Inside Centre with the defence drifting across…)

So long as the plan is agreed by all, it doesn't matter too much which system you use. Above all – at the potential danger spots – you must remove any confusion.

*Does the Winger stay with his opponent or come in to take the extra man?*

*Who covers the Scrum Half break?*

I am a great believer in walking through the defensive plan – on the field of play – and then gradually building up the tempo.

*Defence Running Lines practice: "Backs v. Forwards", Coaching Drills (pages 82/83.)*

## 10. SCRUMMAGING (page 34)

*Scrummaging Laws for this age group prevent the driving scrummage (limit of 1.5 metres.) A far lighter pack can "lock out" reasonably securely against a larger unit so long as body angles and technique are correct. This allows you to pick more of the speedy athletes than hitherto and the game can no longer be totally controlled by the XV with the strongest front five players... That said, it remains highly desirable to have a very powerful front five – especially the two prop forwards... Strong scrummaging is still of crucial psychological value.*

I like to get the set pieces under control first; then I look for organised defence; then I begin the attacking rugby which everyone loves…

i) **Use a scrummage machine** to get the basics right. Footwork and body positions are more easily taught on a solid machine. Once you have the basics, get back to pack v pack scrummaging and put the theory into practice. I like to return to the machine for a regular refresher course, just to check that we are mechanically efficient.

Scrummage practice can be invaluable for building morale amongst the forwards; it is their own mysterious area of expertise and kudos and they need to be good at it…

ii) **Keep things simple.** Coach the **lock out on our own ball and the eight man drive on theirs**. Almost without variation, I aim to lock out and then gather for the secondary drive. In other words, for every ball which we put into the scrum we can expect to drive into the lock and then on command, transfer to an eight man surge.

iii) **Control/discipline.** Although I've never been comfortable with the "blood and thunder" coaching attitude, I do however insist on total discipline. The pack leader must know that he has total concentration from his men and this stems from correct practice on the training ground. I like to work towards 100% focus on the job in hand without too much red mist…

iv) **Endurance v. Snap.** And here lies a gift… Just how far do you stretch your young charges to get the most out of them? Few age-groups will go more willingly to the slaughter if you offer the right incentives. Some coaches insist on building endurance with innumerable repeat scrummages per session – others prefer to keep the load very intensive but less routine… I deal with this complex balance under Fitness and Safety p. 70/71.

## COMPRESSION SCRUMMAGING.

**Coaches will be interested to study the following comments stressed by Richard Greenwood, the former England Coach and Captain:**

*"…There are a number of critical factors which make a complex and physically demanding game easier and more efficient.*

1. If the shoulder platform provided by the front row is low enough, and if, generally speaking, there are eight bottoms below sixteen shoulders… then our scrummage is likely to be efficient.

2. The number of moving parts must be reduced to an absolute minimum. Thus it makes sense to **Lock out**, to lock the legs and to flatten out the backsides of the Second Row and Flankers (who are also part of the Second Row)
Front Row – see later.

3. Binding – perhaps the most important of all… Not onto handfuls of loose shirt but onto the less elastic tops of shorts… So that, with the powerful

inward force of the arms, a collection of eight individuals becomes a cohesive and united force.

We now have a compactly bound unit with a low Front Row shoulder platform with all the studs firmly implanted, which, if nothing else, is not going to go backwards!

### 4. The Front Row Union.

Unsung, and often misunderstood, the Front Row men wage their own private battle…
a) In this area, legs must be flexed at both hip and knees, and not locked as is the case of other forwards…

b) The horizontal back of the Prop Forward acts as a mechanical agent for the transmission of power of the players behind.

c) The props can and must use their legs for more than just balance ie. for forward drive (aided by the inward component of the Flanker's shove.)

### 5. The Link between No 8 and the Tight Head Prop… The Secondary Drive.

After the Lock Out + the winning of the ball (which is now at the feet of the No 8) there comes the timing of the Secondary Drive…

The No 8 sees his Tight Head Prop drop the line of his back a fraction, flexes both knees like a coiled spring. The No 8 can take his cue and call his pack for what comes next… The Prop dips his shoulders and then drives up and through with his legs and back…

**Rest assured that if we got our timing right, squeezed our bindings, flexed our knees and drove at the same time, it would take a tremendous defensive effort by the opposition to stop us going forward…"**

### II. LINEOUT PLAY (page 40)

*At Under 16 level, indeed at any level, Lineout ball, used well, can be even more useful than good scrummage ball; at least you have a bit of space in which to manoeuvre. (At the time of going to print, "lifting" is forbidden at U.15 level.)*
*Even with the Law changes, it remains as much of a lottery as ever, with "winning your own ball" a matter of playing the referee as well as of pure skill.*

In the Player's Guide (p.41) we reluctantly refer to the "trench war-fare" attitude which is needed if we are to prepare our players for the reality of the contest. It is for the referee to judge how precisely he will interpret the letter of the Law…

However the Laws are the Laws… To remove some of the confusion, it helps to look at each part separately:-

### i) The Throw:

Your first and, many would say, the most important decision is to pick your thrower. For some reason, the Hooker usually gets the job and, through constant practice, becomes the best thrower. Some teams like to use the Scrum Half as the thrower, putting a large, aggressive Flanker into the Scrum Half position with various advantages for a forward drive. I don't have a preference and will base any decisions on effectiveness. Whoever you select must be a worker; he needs masses of practice until he can put the ball exactly where his jumpers want it. With the increased importance of lineout ball, this man's task is vital…

Try to instill in the thrower an awareness that throwing-in is a unique personal skill, which he can and must practise. And he can do this alone and without costly equipment…

### ii) Aggressive jumping is essential.

I would not advocate the "Get your retaliation in first" approach but you must motivate your players to "Want the ball" more than the opposition. All the coaching in the world will not win ball for a docile pack. Your pack leader needs to be street wise as well; if your jumpers are small then he will use speed and guile; call short or long lines. On their ball, he must get his men to take on their opponents – perhaps to move one in front of their key jumper. Others in the line must concentrate on getting through the gaps to challenge their Scrum Half and harry him into error.

### iii) The Sweeper.

There are many times when it will be wise to use a sweeper or cleaner-up, rather than tie in your Scrum Half. This involves a forward moving parallel to the lineout to take the ball directly from the jumper. He does not move as the ball leaves the thrower's fingers but judges his move as he sees where the ball is going. There is a serious problem if he moves and then discovers that the opposition has won possession… At junior level, the inclusion of the sweeper certainly aids a weak Scrum Half and allows him to get the ball away; it also slows the transfer down by adding another pair of hands…

### iv) The Blockers.

Referees find this area very difficult to regulate. Close blocking is vital if your jumper is to win controlled ball and the closeness of the support and any lifting must be determined by the referee. The tighter your blockers can get, the more secure the jumper feels… In the existing confusion of lineout play, I teach my players to prepare to "capture the no-man's-land" between the two lines – aware of the simple truth that if we stay back, our opponents certainly won't. There is no alternative but to play to the Referee's rulings in a complex area… (see Drills page 84)

### v) Use of the ball.

Signals need to be understood by everyone. Scrum Half position needs to be thought about… What exactly do you intend to do once you have won the ball?

### 12. RUCK and MAUL (page 45)

*I like to use the set pieces to re-start the game after a break down. Both scrum ball and lineout ball is opposed by an organised defence and, as such, is unlikely to cause our opponents much of a problem. It is in the areas of support play, rucking and mauling that I like to get my players so proficient that they can dominate the game.*

i) **First you aim to be fitter than your opponents**. I see little point in playing the game unless you enjoy the challenge – and fitness work is very much a part of this challenge.

ii) **Next you need to examine running lines** – first on the board and then by walking the moves through on the field. Depth is essential and needs to be understood. Don't all arrive at once, or too flat…

iii) **Who gets there first is crucial. Support play depends on fitness and correct running lines**. The exciting play of today's best Internationals is much to do with the additional pace which large powerful forwards are bringing to the game – recycling the ball at every breakdown and allowing movements to continue even after the tackle.

*Rucking and Mauling Technique is fairly standard to learn but, once taught, it becomes a matter more of will, almost of expectation, than anything else… Your players need to be strong and very confident and this can only be built up by regular practice.*

(Mauling practices are not difficult to set up but I dislike the "raw" rucking practices which have young players smashing into each other in painful fashion. I prefer to use plenty of contact shields, to walk the skill through by numbers and then gradually increase the tempo. Rather like tackling, the "real thing" demands commitment and an element of bravery; it cannot easily be practised "cold".)

*If I had to generalise, I would suggest that with a small pacy pack I would expect to concentrate on the ruck. But the "ruck going forwards and maul when under pressure" is not bad advice for a young team.*

### BASIC RULES for RUCK and MAUL…

Consider the following **Basic Rules** which are common to both the **Ruck** and the **Maul**…

1. **They are both dynamic**, driven forward with low shoulders and leg drive.
Body angle is crucial.

2. **The effort should be concentrated into the narrowest possible area**, aiming for two shoulder widths, and settling for a maximum of three shoulder widths.

3. **Use both inside binding** (so that it is as tight as possible and as close to a scrum as possible) **and outside binding** (so that their fringe players are bound in to give your Half Backs plenty of space.)

4. **There should be no superfluous ball handlers**. The ball is not a plaything and not more than two people should handle.

i) the player who chooses to set up the maul (eg. from a kick-off…)

ii) the player who immediately rips it away, leaving the original ball-carrier at the front or cutting edge of the maul. This second ball-handler either provides the ball direct to the Scrum Half or puts it on the ground for the pack to drive over…

**NB**. It is essential to deliver the ball to the Half Back before the maul has stopped moving forward. Slow, static ball is not quality ball.

5. **In a Ruck, the ball is placed on the ground early** and driven over with the emphasis on both inside and outside binding. If the player in the Scrum Half position chooses (he may be a Second Row forward in the second wave of support) he can "pop the ball" or pick up and drive again. (See **Drills** page 85)

6. **Essential Practice Areas.**
**Going Backwards**…
i) **The deflected ball behind the back of your lineout.**
The first man must fall correctly, secure the ball and drive it immediately forward, giving the support players a target.
ii) **The mid field tackle behind a gain line.**
The nearest player, irrespective of position, must go in immediately, secure the ball and, again, drive it forward giving the arriving support players a target. (**Drills** page 85)

If you are going to encourage a fast rucking style, it is worth re-emphasising the **All Blacks** Coaching guidelines… (also listed in the Young Player book, page 46)

No-one does it better and, executed to a high standard, it sets up the sort of quick ball that all back lines dream of…

*1. Drive beyond the ball.*
*2. Keep on your feet – keep your opponents on their feet.*
*3. Keep your eyes open.*
*4. Bind.*
*5. Come in low – and up.*
*6. Keep your balance.*
*7. Keep your spine "in line".*

Aim for a 2-3-2 formation with the last man standing off (ready for the ball); hook in any other players anywhere near; as players arrive they must bend, bind, drive, with legs pumping hard with short strides – drive in hard – **Rucks Go Forward** – keep a strong firm unit – drive over the ball, leaving it alone for the Scrum Half…

In recent seasons, at senior level, there has been an increase in the use of the **Driving Maul**. Used sensibly, this is a hugely effective ploy and there is no reason why a schoolboy pack should not be capable of reaching a high level of competence. If followed by a dynamic ruck and quick ball for the strike players, it can be devastating at junior or senior level. However, too often in International play it has become an over-used tactic – not particularly attractive to watch and certainly not conducive to the junior 15 man rugby we are hoping to encourage. Technique is all about careful organisation, tightness and body angles.

# Coaching Drills and Practices

**Every coach will include his own Drills.**
**Here are a few which can be used with ambitious young players.**

*With contributions from* **Brian Ashton** *Coach to the Irish XV; Former Bath FC and England Assistant Coach and* **Richard Greenwood** *Former Captain and Coach of the England XV.*

**Including:**

## 1 – HANDLING

### i) PASSING SKILLS.

Based on non-stop shuttle system.
Four groups – one ball – distance between groups varies depending on pressure to be applied.

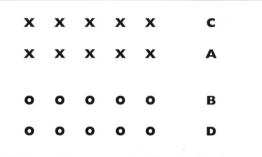

Ball goes from group **A→B→C→D→A**

Variations –
*i) simple flat pass;*
*ii) deep pass – runners delay start;*
*iii) switch or dummy switch;*
*iv) miss one – support outside player;*
*v) first two runners support on the outside;*
*vi) take one player from two groups and have two fixed opposing players;*
*vii) Increase number/decrease restrictions on opposing players.*

### ii) IMPROVING THE BACKS.

Groups of 5, as before. Add two shield holders + a Scrum Half (SH).

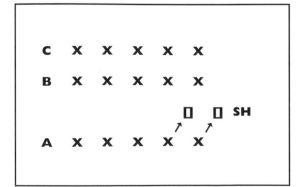

Outside Half takes a flat pass from the SH and gets the ball away under pressure (so does the next attacker).

(When do the outside men begin to run, if they are to inject pace?)

When line A has gone through, the SH and defenders move across to the other side of the grid to defend against line B.
**Progression:** add a third shield.
**Progression:** include a defending back-row to cover across behind shield holders.

## 2 – LINES OF RUNNING

### i) HANDLING.

Group of 4, 5 or 6 players, running off the Coach, as feeder.

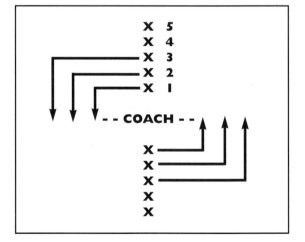

*Key factors:*
i) Hit the ball running straight;
ii) First pass must be flat;
iii) Inside players must preserve space on the outside;

*Progressions:*
i) without opposition;
ii) with fixed opponent;
iii) with drifting opponent(s)…

## ii) SUPPORT PLAY

*Backs and forwards mix together for this type of work...*

**Run in 5 metre channel:**
*i) Coach feeds ball to bunched runners.*
*ii) Ball-carrier always runs down the middle of the channel.*
*iii) There must (as a minimum) be one player to his left, one to his right and one trailing the ball-carrier. i.e. in diamond formation...*

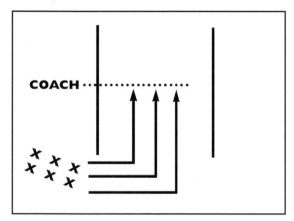

*iv) as each player receives the ball, he goes to the middle and becomes the head of the formation. All the rest adjust.*

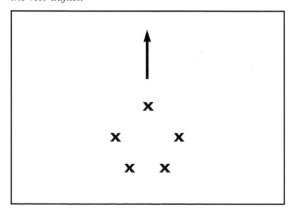

This gives **width** and **depth** to the running.
**Progressions:**
*i) Do it with simple handling;*
*ii) Allow ball-carrier to stop, turn and feed a deep runner;*
*iii) allow ball-carrier to go to ground – this means that two deep runners must pick up the pace of the practice by*

**No 1** straddling the ball and popping it up to
**No 2** who calls and hits the ball at pace...
*(Although used by top-class players in the Senior game, this can easily be adapted for use with Ambitious Young Players...)*

## iii) BACKS v. FORWARDS

*2 v 1, 3 v 2 practices are simple but important.*

If working with a XV, try "**Backs v. Forwards**..."
Backs use it to sharpen their score moves;
Forwards use it to develop the defensive running lines...

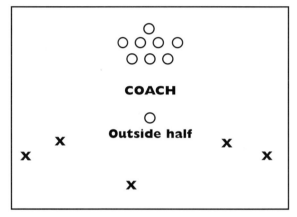

Forwards kneel in Scrummage formation. (I get them on all fours...)
Coach tosses (or rolls) ball to SH and Backs move into attack...
Forwards may move to defend **only** when their number is called. (1 = Back row; 2 = Locks; 3 = front row.)

**Progression:**
Move the scrum closer/wider to make a score more/less likely.
Every "capture" counts 1; every "score" counts 1. First to 5 wins...

## 3 – DECISION MAKING

*Simple to complex…*
*14 players. 2 balls.*

### "4 ATTACKERS v. 3 DEFENDERS":

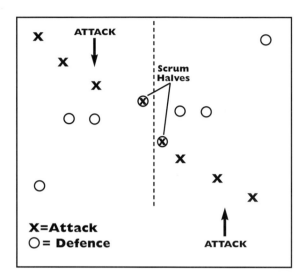

**X=Attack**
**O= Defence**

Attackers operate in a natural cycle and switch with defenders at regular intervals.

*(1.) First two attackers "fix" their men { Important to note: 2 up and 1 back defence.} and release 3A to beat his man using footwork and/or chip kick…*
*(2.) As above to release 3A who takes 3D wide and plays back inside to support runner…*
*(3.) As above to release 3A who brings 3D infield before giving a swivel pass to outside supporting player…*
*(4.) First attacker (1A) fixes first defender (1D) at close quarters and gives a long, flat ball to wing (3A). Play on from there to score…*
*(5.) First two attackers (1A and 2A) dummy switch to release winger (3A). Play on from there to score…*
*(6.) First attacker (1A) fixes first defender (1D). Second defender can stay with his man or drift… Second attacker (2A) makes choice… Play to score…*
*(7.) Both defenders can drift. FB (D3) covers break by the Outside Half (A1); – other attackers work to support.*
*(8.) Defensive FB (D3) closes down space quickly. 2nd Attacker (2A) (Centre…) can chip/grub kick into space behind. Play to score…*

*(These variations operate round two Scrum Halves – and can make a really good, intensive practice with any group of competent players… Organisation is the key.)*

## 4 – CONTACT CYCLE

*5 or 6 players – or more…*

### "PASS, PASS, PENETRATE… "

*i) Nominate a SH.*
*ii) The exercise begins with two passes, then contact (Shield 1);*
*iii) The player who last passed the ball, follows in to support the contact, driving the contact player forwards, rips the ball off and places it on the floor.*
*(iv) Next player becomes SH. Cycle starts again: 2 passes, then contact (Shield 2 or 3…)*

**The practice can be built up by introducing more passes – switch moves – adding a back row &c. Eventually, two teams can practise this way.**

## 5 – THE LINEOUT

*Lineout Assimilation or "Bury the Coach"…*

**This practice is based on the understanding that the *Lineout* is a competitive battle ground. To become successful in this area, players must be able to take care of themselves and of each other. It is a matter of tight, precise team work…**

**Aims:**
1. To produce controlled, quality ball to be passed to a well protected Scrum Half. (In this practice, the Coach…)

2. To provide contact opposition which will test the blocking. Only if the blocking is concentrated and tight will it be possible to prevent the opponents from getting through the line and "burying the Coach"…

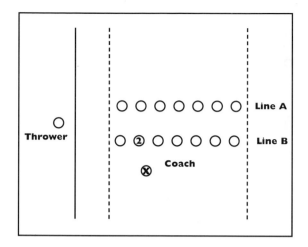

Line A may not jump for the ball. They should try to get **through** the line and "bury the Coach."

**Suggested practice:**
Throw to 2.
Jumpers and support players must work really hard to protect the ball and to ensure that no one comes through the line.
Three jumps, then all players move back one position. Back man comes to the front. This way, all players learn the reality of lineout duties and become more battle hardened and/or street wise. (In no way does this imply the need for law breaking – but it does emphasise the extremely competitive requirements to thrive in the rather lawless zone between the two lines.)

**Progressions.**
Begin without opponents.
Introduce partial contact and build up to full contest.

## 6 – RUCKING AND MAULING

**A. LINEOUT DEFLECTION from back of lineout 15 – 20 m in field.**

Back row player falls, secures, drives forwards (into contact) and is supported by further forwards…
This exposes a workable blind side, with Scrum Half, Hooker/thrower, Outside Half and Blind-side Wing to penetrate and create space for further support play up the touch-line.

Begin with no opposition and gradually introduce…

**B. MIDFIELD RUCK SITUATION inside defending 22, giving a 20 m or so blind side. Ball is driven into the defenders for RUCK BALL.**

Quick ball is taken on the short side, against defending Blind-side Wing and covering forwards…

**C. RUCK/MAUL COMBINATION to score.**

Two groups of defenders: 4 or 5 near the touchline (as for A) and a further 4 or 5 in midfield (as for B above.)

Lineout deflection… Touch-line maul (v. Defence Group 1.) to establish basic possession. Deliver to openside backs.
Drive up field into contact with midfield defenders (Defence Group 2.) Stopped by midfield tackle…
Nearest man secures the ball. Backrow (ie. First support players) decide best use of ball: possibly a "pop up" for fast arriving forwards; possibly a dynamic ruck…
Final surge on to attack/score through broken field with the original defending group covering across to attempt to prevent the try.

## 7 – KICKING PRACTICES

There are those who would restrict kicking for this age group. I prefer to ensure that all players have the basic skills to use if they so wish. With the existing Laws, the very best kickers remain match winners and will need individual guidance from an expert.

**i) Accuracy kicking.**
In pairs or small groups + 1 ball.

Player A kicks along the try line to Player B who is also on the line, but the other side of the posts. The more accurate kickers will be able to bounce the ball off the posts (Place kick) or even put the ball through the posts (Screw kick). The receiver should always start on the line and attempt to catch every kick before it bounces.

Numerous variations are easy to introduce. The practice is both tidy and valuable.

### ii) Power kicking.

Gainers or Force back...
Either 1 v 1, or team v team. One ball or several.

Try to kick the ball over your opponent's line. Kick to be taken from the spot where the last ball was caught. If not caught, from where the ball stopped rolling.
If the ball is kicked out of bounds on the side of the field, the opposing team kicks from the point at which it went out of bounds.

Variations are many.
Use weaker foot; grubber kicks only – along the ground for fielding practice; drop kicks.

Keep the kicking channel quite narrow, giving the opponent(s) a good chance of catching or fielding.

iv. Don't dwell on the ball. Early ball is a powerful weapon.

### Variations:
Begin slowly with Contact pads. Gradually build to more realistic opposition.
Easily altered into a **Mauling Cycle**...

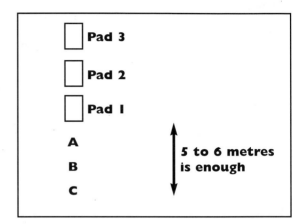

## 8 – BROKEN PLAY & CONTACT CYCLE

*6 players. 1 ball. 3 contact pads.*

**Player A** into Contact Pad 1. Ball to ground.
**Player B** "pops up" to C.

**Player C** into Contact Pad 2. Ball to ground.
**Player A** pops to B.
**Player B** into Pad 3. Ball to ground.
**Player C** pops to A... and repeat.

Runners switch with Pad holders after two complete runs...

Keep run-up distances to no more than 5 or 6 metres...

### Fitness:
The players are pulled by the ball into working much harder than they would without it!

### Coaching points:
i. Attack the ball, not the space wide of the ball-carrier.
ii. Support from depth.
iii. Accelerate the ball on impact. Break the half tackle.

## 9 – TACKLE BAG RELAYS

### BIG HIT PRACTICE

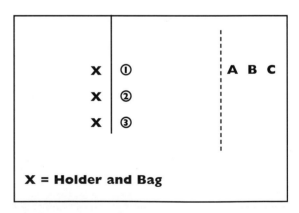

**A hits Bag 1** – and back to line.
**A hits Bag 2** – and back to line.
**A hits Bag 3** – and back to line to set off B.

### Coaching.
I like this simple practice because, as a coach, I can concentrate on one player's technique.
If you are happy about technique and merely want some tackling action, you can allow Player B to start as soon as the bag holder has the first bag back in position after the tackle...